Good Liberals and Great Blue Herons
Land, Labor and Politics in the Pajaro Valley

Good Liberals and Great Blue Herons

Land, Labor and Politics in the Pajaro Valley

Frank Bardacke

Center for Political Ecology
Santa Cruz, California

Published by
The Center for Political Ecology
P.O. Box 8467
Santa Cruz, California 95061
408-459-4541 - phone
408-459-3518 - fax
cns@cats.ucsc.edu - email
http://www.cruzio.com/~cns

Good Liberals and Great Blue Herons:
Land, Labor and Politics in the Pajaro Valley

ISBN 0-9641094-0-9 (only available in paperback)

Photographs are reproduced with the permission of:
Watsonville Register-Pajaronian
Santa Cruz Sentinel

Cover design by Helen Cole
Cover photo by Kurt Ellison

These essays previously appeared in *El Andar*, *Santa Cruz Magazine*, and the *Anderson Valley Advertiser*. Thanks to Julie Miller who read them first, Mike Kostyal who edited most of them, and Barbara Laurence and Jim O'Connor who helped make them into a book.

Contents

Introduction

By Alexander Cockburn

I first met Frank at a *Labor Notes* convention in Detroit, mentioned to him that family business was bringing me out to California's Central Coast and would he have any ideas about where I might live.

He did. The Adobe Motel in Aptos, some two hundred yards from the Pacific, was a place that clearly had seen better days and, as I witnessed over the next couple of years, had worse days ahead. But Frank's judgment was right. I've always had a taste for slightly run-down motels and in upwardly mobile Aptos the Adobe extended a reassuring hand from the past.

Aptos lies in the upper arc of the great curve of Monterey Bay. To its west is Santa Cruz, a few miles up Highway 1. Over the mountains stretches the silicon economy of Santa Clara Valley. Look south, and there in the distance at the end of the lower arc of the bay is the silhouette of Monterey and an industry long gone, Cannery Row. Nearer at hand, some fifteen miles to the east, is the farm town of Watsonville, home to Frank and family these twenty years.

A few years back a French intellectual, Baudrillard by name, drove across the United States, spoke to no one and, having thus rapidly and silently traversed the continent, turned out a book called *America*, which enjoyed considerable success.

Going about the country, driving into a new town, checking out the scene, I often think of Baudrillard careening through landscapes that only time and an expert guide can help one comprehend. Europeans love to repeat that silly line of the expatriate Gertrude Stein about Oakland, "When you get there, there's no there there." Of course Oakland is there, invisible or uninteresting only to those for whom America can be shrunk to a handful of cities genteelly advertised as being on the beaten track.

Often American intellectuals slide into a native version of the same snobbery, believing that thinking, writing or political work can only be conducted in a handful of metropolitan or campus habitats.

What would a Baudrillard or kindred transient make of Watsonville, maybe pulling off Highway 1, looking for a gas stop, heading east on Airport Boulevard, past Hector's, down Freedom Boulevard, along Main, out through some broccoli fields at the south end of town and then without further ado back on 1 with Castroville, artichoke heart of the world, next up on the route map.

The glazed tourist's eye might, even at a speed never dropping below 30 mph, pick out a few of the insignia of local drama: a church without a steeple, some of the south end of Main missing altogether. Watsonville got hit pretty bad in the earthquake of 1989.

But even at a walking pace it's hard to decipher the main streets and side alleys without detour and patient investigation. Take those snug-looking, single-story Maybeck houses. How many families are crammed in them? Two? Three? More? And the broccoli cutters, a raggedy line of figures in the middle distance. You can't tell anything about them at that range, unless through their old cars, sometimes their homes, parked nearer at hand. How much are they making? Where are they from?

In the pieces in this book Frank gives the answers, same way they should be given for every town in America but almost never are. It's not easy to be a truthful, therefore radical reporter about the significant affairs of a town where — to use one of Frank's favorite images from Ivan Illich — you can see the surrounding fields from the church steeple. The man you criticized in harsh terms yesterday is the man you meet on Main Street tomorrow.

You have to know what you're talking about. A reporter can make a mess of the street names in Mogadishu and be safe enough from rebuke. Err on a name, an event, a deal, a saga in Watsonville and your critics are outside the door or next in line at the post office.

That's why most local journalism is so unselfconsciously deadly, or if self-conscious, so sentimental in the manner of Garrison Keillor. It's also why, when you read Frank or the *Anderson Valley Advertiser,* put out by Bruce Anderson two hundreds miles further north in Mendocino County, you can understand the explosive political potential of robust description and analysis of locality. It's America's great lack.

Frank has a funny passage in his Autobiographical Note at the end of this collection where he describes how *El Andar* — which published most of these pieces — was the eighth alternative publication he's worked with, starting with *The Wooden Shoe* in 1962 in Berkeley with Marvin Garson, on to *Root and Branch* with Ruth Markovitz, Robert Scheer and Maurice Zeitlin and thence by a zigzag route to *El Obrero* in Salinas, "no obscure titles now; we were straightforwardly proletarian revolutionaries. This monthly tabloid lasted two seasons until our five-member collective split in three different directions and I landed feet down in the friendly confines of Watsonville."

So, across the next twenty years, he got to know the place, just as he would have gotten to know Stockton, which was another long-term settlement Frank once told me he and his wife Julie Miller considered back in the early 1970s. If things had gone another way, we'd now know much more about Stockton.

As it is, Frank learned how Watsonville works and how the farm land works and how the two evolve, according to the motions of the world economy. This is no book of closed horizons. At the other end of Main Street is Michoacán, whence so many of the workers came; is Irapuato whither so many of the jobs finally went; is London where some of the momentous recent decisions in the history of Watsonville were made.

Frank learned these things and he explains them to us: the local in terms of the global and vice versa. "Urban renewal"? Try Frank's account of what happened to the 200 block on Main, or how the city planners saw their chance after the earthquake of '89. Liberalism? Read about the blue herons. International capital? Follow the struggles of the Green Giant workers.

Back in the 1930s the Federal Writers' Project of the WPA produced the last attempt at a detailed guide to America. The volumes vary. Even though the guides were in part written by radicals in the depths of the Depression, class politics were entirely suppressed. In the California volume, you can find amusing entries for Aptos, and for Watsonville, and for the Pajaro Valley, the river of the bird so named, the guide says, "because they (the Portola expedition) found on its banks a great eagle stuffed with straw by the Indians....it is a vast sweep of apple orchards....Watsonville's Plaza in the center of town was the scene of bull and bear fights and horse races were held in its main street in the days when the townsmen spent their Sundays — after dutiful attendance at early mass — gambling, dancing, and racing."

That's about the best the zealously censored or self-censoring WPA writers could do, never rising above the level of the anecdotal. Imagine guides to American states written by people like Frank! A guide that told tourists gliding down Highway 1 who owns those fields, who the workers are and what happened to their union, their town, their lives. A guide that had humor, but also passion and politics.

With such a guide in hand those visitors could decode Main Street, understand why no low income housing got built along Route 129, visit the Madonna of the oak grove and know its origins back in Indian time.

A sense of time. Nothing stands still in Frank's Watsonville. The fingers of the world economy shape and reshape its destinies. The town's polar attraction shifts from the southward pull of Salinas, to the valley of silicon an hour's drive north. One of Frank's central themes here is the movement of history, the fateful swerves of political economy.

"Imported water, argues Ivan Illich in his book *H2O and the Waters of Forgetfulness*, converted Rome from a city to an Empire....The Empire was built and the city was lost. Imported water will not transform Watsonville into an Empire. But it will fully integrate us into the Hydraulic Empire of the American West. And it will destroy the Pajaro Valley as a place."

Thus does Frank take us from Rome to Watsonville, in a marvelous swoop of political ecology. Let this be the one that instructs the other guides that hopefully will follow. There can be no better model.

Petrolia, California, August, 1993

v

Preface

Putting Watsonville on the Map

I found my favorite map of Watsonville in a little book, *La Casa Dividida*, about Gómez Farías, Michoacán. In the middle 1980s, the author, Gustavo Lopez Castro, counted a grand total of 448 extended families in Gómez, more than 80 percent of whom regularly send migrants to the United States, most of them coming to Watsonville. This migration started with mule drivers in the 19th century, picked up speed with the Mexican Revolution, and became the standard way of life for *los Gomeños* after World War II, as whole families started to move back and forth across, what for them had become, a somewhat fictitious border.

The map, in the back of the book, is a simple drawing of more than 1,500 miles of California and Mexican coast line, with black dots positioning the six important cities in the lives of the people of Gómez Farías: from south to north, Gómez Farías, Guadalajara, Tijuana, Los Angeles, Watsonville, San Francisco. It is a map for a Watsonville chauvinist, of which I am one of the worst, placing our town of 30,000 souls in proper perspective.

An earlier map helped recruit me to Watsonville. I found it in 1971, the year I left Berkeley, when I was living in Salinas.

I was with Julie at North Salinas High where she wanted to look over some books for young children at what publishing companies call a "Teachers' Fair." Wandering through the stalls, I came across a series of color overlays which showed where California's fresh fruits and vegetables are grown. Watsonville was right there in big letters, and I remember dropping the overlays one by one—amazed as colorful drawings of strawberries, apples, blackberries, lettuce, and celery appeared over the name of what I then knew to be only a neighboring town next to the sea.

The last map I helped make myself. I cut out, pieced together, and pasted on poster board three sections of the Army Corp of Engineers' Transverse Mercator Projection of the Western United States. It is a three-dimensional map with the vertical scale half the horizontal scale (the surface of the earth is really quite flat, and only by exaggerating heights can a map give some sense of what hills and mountains look like to human beings). I put it together so that it extends from Madera in the San Joaquin Valley in the east, to 100 miles into the Pacific Ocean in the west; and from San Ardo, 75 miles down the Salinas Valley to the southeast, up to the San Rafael-Richmond bridge across San Francisco Bay, 100 miles northwest. Watsonville is in the center (it is my map!) huddled in the Pajaro Valley, enclosed on two sides by the southern tip of the Santa Cruz mountains, on a third side by the beginning of the Gabilan range, with the fourth side facing the Pacific.

The map tells a chilling story. Running parallel to the Salinas Valley is the Santa Clara Valley, a half hour drive over the hills from Watsonville. On the map little green dots were used to represent orchards, and the Santa Clara Valley in 1967 is all green dots, from Gilroy to Morgan Hill to San Jose. In the 25 years since, the orchards have all gone. Some of what this book is about is my attempt, together with other people, to protect what remains of the little green dots in the Pajaro Valley. And to build the political power necessary to make our own map of what Watsonville might look like 25 years hence.

But this is not a geography book. It is a book about politics—and Watsonville's political history is nearly as rich as its top soil. Since the 1930s, Watsonville workers (Filipinos, Mexicans, Anglos) have been the militant core of several farmworker movements. The 1934 and '36 strikes in Watsonville and Salinas—involving an uneasy, and eventually, betrayed alliance between Filipinos in the fields and Anglos in the lettuce sheds—were among the largest strikes in California agricultural history. Some thirty years later, a Watsonville wildcat of Mexican workers sparked the victorious 1970 United Farmworkers Union (UFW) strike in the Salinas Valley, and even in a period of decline the UFW remains stronger in Watsonville and Salinas than anywhere else.

Watsonville had such a reputation as a fighting, working class town that John Steinbeck set his Depression-era morality tale, *In Dubious Battle*, here in the Pajaro Valley, although in an affront to topography he changed our name and moved us to the San Joaquin Valley. More than a thousand local frozen-food workers lived up to that militant reputation just a few years ago when they fought local bosses to a standstill in an 18-month strike in which no strikers crossed the picket line.

A year after that strike ended—I think of it as a tie, the workers saved their union contract, but accepted a wage cut—Watsonville was again on the national political map. In July, 1988, the 9th U.S. Circuit Court of Appeals in San Francisco decided that a recent United States Supreme Court decision required the City of Watsonville to change from at-large to district elections. The suit had been filed by the Mexican American Legal Defense Fund, which picked Watsonville as a test case because the lack of Mexican-American representation in city politics had been so outrageous. Watsonville, a binational, bicultural town since the massive immigration of Mexicans in the 1960s, had elected, in all its history, but one Mexican-American to its city council.

It was just as the appeals court announced its decision promising Mexican Watsonville some representation in city politics that I began writing the essays collected in this book. I think of them as extended leaflets; most were written in the midst of particular political campaigns. I meant them to be not only a map of the territory, but an informal guide to political action. I have the same immodest hope for this book: that it will help people think about what they should do.

(January, 1994)

Labor

Anita Contreras leading frozen food workers' march *(Photo: UPI)*

1

Our Lady of the Live Oak

"In some parts of Mexico, the Virgin of Guadalupe is still addressed by her Indian name." — Ena Campbell, *The Virgin of Guadalupe and the Female Self Image*

People use that name, Tonantzin, right here in Watsonville, out by the sacred oak tree. She probably crossed the border by the light of the moon. Brought by a coyote no doubt. Not the kind you pay, but the one, who along with Eagle, created Pinto Lake and the whole rest of the world. It must have been a testy night. The Virgin and the Coyote.

Miracles happen when people need them, sometimes. Necessity does not have an only child, she is the mother of all kinds of creatures. Always.

In 1531, ten years after Cortez, his soldiers and his Indian allies destroyed Tenochitlan, the original people of what is now Mexico needed a miracle. Their city had been razed, high priests tortured and killed, their temples systematically destroyed. They were dying in such great numbers—succumbing to European disease, weapons, and organization —that in the space of 25 years about four out of every five would be dead.

A young Franciscan priest, soon to become the First Archbishop of New Spain, Juan de Zumarraga, also needed a miracle. Cortez's homicidal search for treasure was sanctioned by the Cross, of course, but if the fury of his mission continued unchecked, there wouldn't be any souls left for the

Church to save, not to mention hands and backs to work the fields and mines. Zumarraga sided with those within the church who argued that the Indians had souls and were capable of salvation. Their opponents, civil authorities in New Spain and high ecclesiastical officials back in Europe, maintained that the Indians were not as fully human as the European *gente de razón*, and were destined to be slaves. The debate would rage for more than fifty years.

Just one month after Zumarraga was made Bishop, Guadalupe appeared. This was quite a stroke of luck — as a Bishop, Zumarraga had the authority to immediately validate the vision as an authentic miracle. It is a lovely story, and many have told it before me, but none as well as the Indian Antonio Valeriano, who wrote the first account in his native Nahuatl in 1533, just two years after the miracle.

As Valeriano tells it, Juan Diego, a recently baptized Indian, was walking on the hill of Tepeyac when Guadalupe first materialized.

"He heard...a sweet and beautiful singing which sounded to him like a multitude of different birds singing together softly and in harmony, singing back and forth in chorus in a wonderful concert, whose echoes resounded and were amplified by the high mountain rising above the little hill....In the midst of that brightness he saw a most beautiful Lady....her garments were shining so brightly that striking the rough boulders rising above the hilltop, it made them seem like carved transparent precious stones."

She called herself the Virgin Mary, Mother of God, and told Juan Diego to go to the Bishop and tell him to build her a church on the hill of Tepeyac. But, so the story goes, Zumarraga was suspicious of Juan Diego and his vision. Our "poor and humble" Indian returned to the hill a second time. He told the Virgin to send someone more important to talk to the Bishop. But Guadalupe rejected the advice, explaining that she had purposefully picked one like him for this mission, and sent him back to try again.

The good Bishop was still suspicious and told Juan Diego to return with some proof that the Virgin had appeared to him. Juan Diego was ashamed to go back to the Virgin and make such a request, so he tried to avoid the place where he had seen the vision. But as fortune would have it, Juan Diego's uncle fell sick, and Juan Diego had to go on an emergency errand past that very same hill, and once again she appeared to him. This time the Virgin asked him to pick some roses in a spot where normally only desert plants grow, and then she put the roses into the Indian's cloak, and told him to take them to the Bishop.

When Juan Diego undid the cloak to show Zumarraga the roses, the image of the Virgin was stamped upon it. Zumarraga and Juan Diego had their miracle.

But it wasn't quite that easy. Zumarraga's enemies in the Church were quick to point out that Tepeyac was the hill that belonged to the Aztec mother/fertility goddess, Tonantzin, and they claimed that the devious and idolatrous Indians were only pretending to worship the Virgin so that they could continue to sing and dance to their old goddess. A second doctrinal battle raged in New Spain, with the lower, poorer village priests promoting Guadalupe/Tonantzin as a way of winning the Indians to Christianity (it also helped that if you didn't convert, you might be thrown in the nearest volcano) and the older, higher Church hierarchy denouncing her as a pagan idol.

But the miracle was the perfect solution, a model for the combination of Indian paganism and European Catholicism which was to become the new popular religion of Mexico. Eventually in 1754, a Papal Bull formally declared Guadalupe to be "Patroness and Protector of New Spain."

And so she remains today, especially in Mexico, where Hidalgo made her part of his famous grito ("Long Live the Virgin of Guadalupe and Down with the Government!"), Zapata's troops carried her image into battle, and the shape of her famous mantle can be seen on everything from *pulquerias* (the nectar of the Maguey is believed by many to be the milk from her breast) to cradle-boards, Kleenex boxes, and even to that part of Mexico so close to home, a live oak tree, *Quercus agrifolia*, at Pinto Lake County Park, just outside Watsonville.

The famous shape of Guadalupe's mantle appears about twenty feet up on a main branch of a middle-aged coast live oak. She is the dark wood (as befits one of the world's most famous Dark Madonnas) and her outline is formed by the lighter bark that surrounds her. The play of dark and light bark creates designs all over the tree, many of them not unlike the semi-official image, but this bothers the pilgrims not at all. It is the entire tree that's holy.

On a recent Saturday morning, I joined a couple dozen others — all Mexicans, mostly women — at the foot of Our Lady, guessing at the shapes. (Tens of thousands have visited since she first appeared on June 17, 1992.)

"Look there, can't you see Her?"

"Oh, now I see Her. Yes. Definitely."

"And behind Her is the Cross."

A man has picked up one of the large mirrors from the picnic table in front of the tree, and is using it to reflect the sun on all the sacred spots. Also on the table is a music book, a dollhouse-sized miniature church, and a petition to the county asking that this spot be protected as a sacred shrine.

"There are supposed to be little angels on this branch, but I don't see them."

4

"Last week someone saw the face of Jesus over there."

"Yes, yes, I can make it out! But the crown is not complete."

It is a warm fall morning. No fog. From our spot at the picnic table we overlook a small inlet of the lake, where American coots, mallards and red-winged blackbirds raise — well, not quite the symphony that Juan Diego heard — but the chirps and shrieks of life. Across the inlet on the middle peninsula of the lake are clumps of eucalyptus, a few willows, second-growth redwoods and a lovely broad leaf maple.

But basically we are in an oak grove. The oak was the Tree of Life to the Ohlone, under which they prayed, danced, and sang just before the acorn harvest. The Calendaruc, the Pajaro Valley triblet of the Ohlone language group, harvested acorns by the shores of Pinto Lake, and as coast live oaks live up to 500 years, they probably worshipped under a tree whose acorn formed the very oak under which people worship today.

Not that the Ohlones have a monopoly on oak tree worship. The name Druid means "knowers of the oak" and, as mythologists Robert Graves and George Frazier pointed out long ago, oak groves have been sacred places throughout Europe since before recorded history. Oaks are trees of the gods, places of worship and sacrifice.

Back to our sacred grove. A woman with a Polaroid camera is taking pictures of various parts of the tree and then closely inspecting the results.

"Look here," she shows me, "can you see the face of the sacred dog?"

She kisses the picture and adds it to the stack on the picnic table.

The fence, built by the park attendants to protect the tree from its devotees, is covered with tokens, as is the base of the tree itself. Rosaries, neckties, photos of loved ones, drivers' licenses, student identification cards, green cards, a picture of Joe Montana, ribbons, Mexican flags, a dried ear of corn, notes to Our Lady, and flowers, hundreds of flowers both real and plastic, all together make the shrine.

Two prayers catch my attention. Both are in Spanish. One is written in ink, on a fading piece of paper.

"I pray to you for the health of my father's head, my mother's hand, and to be cured of my disease that only you know about."

The other, professionally done on a plastic card, is about "Our Lady of the Americas."

"Do not worry about anything.
Am I not here?
I who am your Mother
Are you not under my protection?"

At mid-morning, Anita Contreras Mendoza arrives. There is a stir in the small crowd, for it is Anita who first saw Our Lady of the Live Oak appear out of a cold wind, ensconced in a sea shell, dressed not in the splendid jewels seen by Juan Diego, but in the ordinary clothes of a farmworker. She was like "*una campesina valiente*," Anita says.

I have known Anita for a long time. She and her sister, Esperanza, were two of the most important rank-and-file leaders of the 1985 cannery workers' strike. It was the strength and internal solidarity of the Mexican women strikers, like Anita and Esperanza, which enabled the Teamsters to survive Watsonville Canning's attempt to bust the local union.

During the strike Anita's faith helped keep her strong. At one crucial meeting when the strikers decided to continue their struggle despite the objections of the Teamster International, Local 912, and their own strike committee, Anita and Esperanza led the way.

"To stop now would be giving up," Anita said, "as long as God is in his Heaven, I will never give up."

Three days later, just before she lead the procession on her knees to St. Patrick's Church, which was the symbolic end of the victorious wildcat that concluded the 18-month strike, she said to the press,

"I now go down on my knees before God, but I go on my knees before no man."

Anita has been just as strong about the social and political meaning of her vision. The apparition remains on the tree she says, "so people don't kill, don't hit their wives, don't abuse their children, and to help them find the truth."

After hugs all around, Anita leads a half-hour recital of the rosary. The recitation of prayers includes the singing and rhythmic clapping of a small chorus of women. The words of the prayer are mournful, but the music is upbeat. Throughout the recitation, Our Lady literally shines, as the peoples' mirrors reflect the sun's light onto the dark bark that represents her form.

I am godless, an atheist to the very depths of my shallow soul. But in the Year of Our Lord, 1992, it would seem that we have failed to live up to Nietzsche's challenge. His acknowledgement of the death of God (he merely recognized it, he said, he didn't cause it) was meant to dare people to construct our own moralities and then try to live by them, without the aid of an external, otherworldly authority. Today you would be hard put to find moral order in the secular world. The market and the bottom line decide the difference between right and wrong. The apparent failure of the socialist project has only made matters worse. When you talk morality today, you end up sounding like a preacher.

7

This failure of secular morality is the philosophical basis of the theology of liberation that has swept through Latin America in the last thirty years. (Its material basis was the brutal repression of all alternative political and moral choices, driving the poor into the Church as the only place they could legally organize.) But in order for the liberation theologists to make the Catholic Church an activist agent of social change, they had to rewrite some basic Catholic doctrine.

The Hebrew intellectuals and Greek mathematicians who invented the solitary God placed him high in the sky, away from the world, where eventually he became an abstract principle (the solution to certain philosophical riddles) rather than a personality. The Christians brought God back down to earth. Deities (Jesus himself, the Saints, the multiplying Madonnas) once again walked among us in this world. At the same time, however, in a mysterious contradiction, Christianity changed God's promise from the worldly, earth-bound goal of liberation and justice, to the private, otherworldly goal of personal salvation. The Christians brought God closer, but placed his promise further away.

The idea of everlasting life, what Nietzsche called, "the most contemptible of all unrealizable promises, the impudent doctrine of person immortality," does not appear in the Old Testament. The Jews believed that when you are dead, you're dead. God did not grant universal salvation; rather he delivered a particular people from slavery. Christ's main deviation from Jewish canon was his pledge of life after death, that the ultimate relief from human suffering was not here in this world, but in the next.

This presented quite a doctrinal problem for those Latin American priests whose commitment to the poor compelled them to political action. They solved the puzzle by reinterpreting two of the basic ideas of Catholicism: sin and salvation.

Sin was redefined to be societal as well as personal. It was not primarily a consequence of flawed human nature, but of certain specific social relations. An unjust society, the actual situation of contemporary Latin America, was understood as being sinful. And, perhaps even more importantly, salvation now meant a people's liberation from injustice. Catholic salvation had always been (with a few exceptions) individual, private, universal, and otherworldly. Liberation theologists made salvation collective, public, historical, and very much of this world. Turning Catholicism on its head, they argued that the goal of religious practice was to bring the Kingdom of God to this world.

All very metaphysical to be sure, but metaphysics mixed with the very material struggles of the peoples of Latin America. What a historical surprise that organizers in the slums of Brazil, revolutionaries in Nicaragua, guerrillas in El Salvador, activists in Mexico City, argue not so much about Marxist "stages of development," but rather about the meaning of the Gospel.

Just how seriously do people take these ideas? In 1982, a Guatemalan Protestant Minister, Mario Carrillo Ortíz, was arrested along with some 40 others on suspicion of being a guerrilla sympathizer. Afterwards, Carrillo Ortíz reported in the magazine *Polémica* that during the interrogation/torture, one of the questions thrown at the prisoners was this: Is Christ a Savior or a Liberator? The wrong answer earned you a blow to the head.

Perhaps Our Lady of the Live Oak is both Savior and Liberator. She fortifies people like Anita who fight for justice; she delivers God's mercy to the young lady who suffers a secret disease. Here in Watsonville, with our relatively low level of struggle compared to the jungles of Guatemala, we can still have it both ways.

We have had our share of local fights, however, and many of these struggles have been fought in religious as well as secular language. Also, in the last decade, there have been many attempts by low-level church authorities in Monterey and Santa Cruz counties to set up local *comunidades de base* — the basic organizational unit of Liberation Theology in Latin America. But these small groups of lay Catholic believers using the Gospel as a guide to political action have not taken hold in the Pajaro Valley. Instead we have a few socially active nuns and seminarians working together with individual believers, immersed in our local culture of Mexican folk piety. Will the border crossing of Guadalupe/Tonantzin help those who again are trying to establish a local Catholic-based community organization? Or is she a diversion, religious consolation for some and a sideshow for others? God only knows.

(December, 1992)

Irrigator (*Photo: Kurt Ellison/Register-Pajaronian*)

2

Adiós, West Coast Shorty

As I walk down Prospect Street to Lulu's to get my morning paper, occasionally I see Mitch Resetar. Mitch is one of Watsonville's serious walkers; well over six feet tall, he leans forward from the waist, vigorously pumps his arms, and strides out at a speed to rival some of our best Sunday joggers. Head down, self-absorbed, he walks the streets talking to himself.

Once I stopped him, wishing, I suppose, to be a part of that conversation. It was hard to flag him down. I had to yell, "hey Mitch" several times, but when he finally stopped and turned, he seemed neither annoyed nor in a hurry, and he gave our small encounter his full attention.

He asked me where I was working now, and how I liked it, and then, much to my surprise, he asked after my wife and oldest daughter, by *name*. I asked about his walking and his health, and we were done. Neither one of us mentioned the time, some 16 years ago, when we stood in one of his lettuce fields, chest to chest like baseball manager and umpire, screaming insults at each other, daring the other man to be the first to strike a blow.

Oh, to be inside Mitch's head as he walks the streets of Watsonville. Mitch's grandfather, Mike, arrived in San Fran-

13

cisco from Cilipe, near Dubrovnik, Croatia, in 1901, at the very beginning of this God-awful century. He worked at what he could find, and then, the story goes, he made his way down to Watsonville where he earned some money picking apples. Not a fruit tramp for long, he quickly figured out that in San Francisco he could sell Watsonville apples for a lot more money than he was being paid to pick them. According to the family myth, he used his meager savings to buy the right to harvest one tree, and then a second and a third, until he and his two brothers had built a Pajaro Valley empire. By mid-century their holdings included West Coast Farms, the Resetar Hotel, and Watsonville Exchange, all of which made the Resetar family the largest employer in Santa Cruz County.

Add the stories of the other Slavonian families (Scurich, Franich, Letunich, Pavlovitch, it's a long list), throw in a couple of Italians (Crosetti and Console), and you have the history of Watsonville's ruling class from the 1920s to the 1960s. They all lived in town — the Yugoslavs modestly, hiding their wealth, the Italians flaunting it outrageously — and they built and cared for local government and schools, shaping the community to meet their own interests.

Although still present, these families no longer rule. The people who now make the fundamental decisions that shape our community no longer live in town. They issue their commands from plush offices on the top floors of massive buildings made of steel and tinted glass, in cities like Los Angeles, Chicago, and London. Their names and faces are unrecognized on our streets: David Murdock, Kenneth Douglas, Stanley Grimstead. They head giant corporations— Castle & Cooke, Dean Foods, and Grand Metropolitan—that will stay here as long as it is profitable, and will leave when they can make more money someplace else.

I don't mean to romanticize the old, down home rulers, and the passing of the old order. When Mitch Resetar and I were screaming at each other, the issue was the continued use of that back-breaking tool, West Coast shorty, *el cortito*, the short-handled hoe.

I was working for Mitch at West Coast Farms, thinning lettuce at the time. The state legislature, after years of pressure by the UFW and other farm worker advocates, had just passed a law making the short-handled hoe illegal. One morning, after telling disbelieving workers about the law, I asked the foreman to bring us the legally required long-handled hoes. He answered that, as usual, I was full of shit, and that it would be impossible to thin lettuce with a long-handled hoe. But after a few days of my incessant harping on the subject, and after some friends of mine distributed a leaflet throughout the Pajaro and Salinas Valleys publicizing the new law, we got some action.

As work was about to begin one morning in a sunken field off San Juan Road, and after the foreman opened the compartment under the bus where they kept the short-handled hoes, a higher-up in the company arrived in a pickup truck, with a half dozen long-handled hoes in the bed. It was carefully explained to us that we had the option to use a long-handled hoe if we liked, but whoever used one must not fall behind the rest of the crew.

As if on cue, some of the workers picked up their short-handled hoes and raced to the field. I urged others to join me in trying the other model, but no one did. I looked over the hoes in the truck bed. The sorriest looking bunch of tools I have ever seen in my life, they looked like rejects from the tool section of the local Goodwill: broken handles, rusted steel, chipped blades. I picked up the best one I could find and started out.

I was a slow worker anyway—it took me about four seasons in the fields to work up to average speed—and soon I was far, far behind the rest of the crew. The foreman was on my case; according to him, if I couldn't keep up with the others I would be fired. I answered that it was illegal to fire me for using a long-handled hoe, and that instead of harassing me, he ought to get a hoe himself and help me catch up.

That afternoon Mitch Resetar arrived. I did not know that he owned the company, but I could see from the way the other workers watched him that he was an important man, and I soon learned that he was there to put me in my place.

That is when our shouting match began. He screaming that the long-handled hoe was only an "option," and that I had to keep up with the rest of the workers; and I screaming back that the short-handled hoe was illegal, and that nobody should be using it. The rest of the crew stopped and watched as we stood in the middle of the fields yelling in each other's face.

No, the old order was no sweet thing. The short-handled hoe is perhaps the best symbol of its reign: wealth for the local bosses made at the expense of the broken bodies of two generations of Filipino and Mexican farm workers.

But at least the bosses lived in town, a town the best of them cared about. And occasionally some of them could be made to confront the consequences of their rule.

Fat chance we have to scream at Stanley Grimstead about what he has done to Watsonville through his decision to fire 400 Green Giant workers. Mr. Grimstead, CEO and chairman of the board of Grand Metropolitan, lives far away in London in his own world of transnational corporate intrigue, fully isolated from the people he affects, shielded from the misery wrought by his corporate policies.

There is one thing wrong with this argument. Although distant corporations now make Watsonville's crucial production decisions, they have not bought our local land. Castle & Cooke, corporate owners of Bud Antle, who now use the fields which Mitch Resetar's defunct West Coast Farms used to farm, own little land in the Pajaro Valley. They choose to lease it instead. This arrangement seems to fit the needs of both the transnationals (who want to stay as mobile as possible) and the local landlords, who now make their money from property management, real estate speculation, and rent.

So our landlords are still local. A few of them are good, decent people, but many of them earn scandalous rents off of living conditions almost impossible to believe. These conditions are revealed to the general public only through natural or human disasters: earthquakes or fires which show people living 13 to a room, a couple dozen using a single toilet.

When I stop Mitch Resetar in the street to pass the time of day, I suspect I make a silent call to these local landlords. I want to remind him — and his fellow Slavonians — that they come from a tradition of struggle unmatched in modern Europe. For more than a thousand years, the hopelessly outnumbered Croatians, Serbs, Macedonians, and Slovenians have protected their cultures against some of the most powerful empires the world has ever known: the Ottoman Empire from the Southeast, the Austrian-Hungarian Empire from the Northeast, the German Nazis and Italian fascists from the West and Northwest, and the Russian Empire from the North.

Now, these peoples' second home, the Pajaro Valley, is threatened by a New Empire — the transnational corporations of the late 20th century. Will our local Slavonians make a pact with Mexican and working class Watsonville to similarly protect what is valuable in the small town culture of the Pajaro

Valley? Wouldn't the basis of that pact be a commitment to justice for the Mexican farm workers who helped them make their wealth? Will they join us, for example, in an alliance to convert the airport to low cost housing, as a first step in the struggle for a better life for the vast majority of the people of the Pajaro Valley?

Right after our shouting match ended and Mitch Resetar left the lettuce field on San Juan Road, someone else on the crew picked up a long-handled hoe and started to use it. Within a week all the available long-handled hoes were being used, and the rest of the workers were agitating for more. In two weeks the company had provided new long-handled hoes for everyone.

I like to believe that Mitch was not so much frightened by the legal complications of the situation, as he was determined, finally, to do the right thing.

(August, 1990)

Box of frozen vegetables packed in Mexico *(Photo: Joe Fahey)*

Mexican frozen vegetables being unloaded at Shaw subsidiary *(Photo: Joe Fahey)*

3

THANKS, But No Thanks

This is a story of fraud. Big time fraud in our little town. In April, 1986, Richard Shaw started an organization called THANKS (Together Helping Americans Nationwide Keep Strong). Its stated purpose was to "identify and promote the purchase of all American-grown farm products." Shaw began the campaign using himself as the main weapon. He travelled the country promoting the THANKS label and warning consumers that cheap, possibly contaminated, Mexican agricultural imports were ruining "our" farmers and threatening the nation's health. He proudly proclaimed that under his direction, starting in 1986, Shaw Frozen Foods canceled all its foreign contracts and now bought only from American growers.

Surely, almost everyone in Watsonville heard this line. It was widely covered in the local press and endorsed by nearly every organization in town. The problem is that since its inception, the THANKS crusade has been a lie. Shaw Frozen Foods has bought and packed frozen Mexican broccoli and cauliflower from 1986 until the plant was bought by Dean Foods this year, and Dean Foods continues to do the same.

In the winter of 1986, about nine months after Richard

Shaw founded THANKS, I heard for the first time that the Shaw plant was still packing Mexican vegetables. My old friend, Joe Fahey, then a Teamster Local 912 business agent and now the Local's President, told me this. He said he had been told by many workers at Shaw that they had seen boxes of frozen cauliflower and broccoli marked "product of Mexico" being dumped on the processing lines. He then asked some frozen-food employers in town who confirmed the story, saying that all local packers run Mexican products.

But Joe had no physical proof, he hadn't seen the boxes himself, and nobody was willing to "go public." At that point, the story remained unsubstantiated rumor.

Several months later, Joe shot the two photographs on page 20. He took them on June 17, 1987, at Farmers' Cold Storage, a small frozen-food operation on the end of Kearney Street, which Richard Shaw and a few others bought after the frozen food strike ended. Farmers' Cold Storage operated as a non-union subsidiary of the Shaw plant and Joe was over there talking to a couple of Shaw mechanics who had been sent from the main plant to work on some equipment.

While he was there he saw a trailer of 30-pound boxes of cauliflower clearly marked "product of Mexico" being dumped by a small crew into unmarked tote bins, which were then being loaded onto a Shaw flatbed truck. Joe recognized this flatbed as the one that regularly runs back and forth between Farmers' Cold Storage and Shaw.

Joe asked one of the workers for an empty box, and then rushed to Ford's to buy a camera and film. He returned and took several photographs before people from the Farmers' Cold Storage office chased him off the lot.

For the next few months Joe showed the pictures around, telling his story to frozen food employers, union officials, THANKS associates, and his friends. It became an industry joke: Fahey caught Shaw packing Mexican products.

One of the people Joe told was me. He knew I was interested. Since early in the frozen food strike I have been arguing to whomever would listen that the statistics on imported Mexican frozen vegetables are misleading. The local frozen bosses have used these statistics to explain their troubles and as a justification for the massive pay cuts they forced on the workers during the strike. The statistics show that Mexican imports are taking a larger and larger share of the American market. But what the industry does not say is that the vast majority of Mexican imports come to the United States in bulk form, and then are repacked by domestic frozen food firms. Such imports often are not in direct competition with domestic production; they are an integral part of it. The pay cuts were not caused by Mexican imports; they were a consequence of the balance of forces between labor and capital here in Watsonville.

Joe let me have a copy of the pictures; I showed them to a few friends and repeated Joe's story around town. When Shaw sold his plant to Dean Foods (about a month after Joe took the pictures) the story lost some of its impact and I let it drop. It became just one of Watsonville's semi-secrets, another delicious small town story that runs completely counter to the official "news."

That is why I am printing it now. As another reminder that the "official story"—the one you read in the *Register-Pajaronian*, the *San Francisco Chronicle* and sometimes even the *Santa Cruz Sun*—is often wrong, and wrong in such ways as to fit the interests of the strong. This was never more true than the local coverage of the Watsonville frozen food strike. It was the strike, and the employers' successful campaign to blame everything on Mexican imports, that gave birth to the THANKS fraud. The import statistics were convenient for almost everyone but the workers themselves: the employers who forced the pay cuts, the union officials who accepted them, and those parts of the Left who wanted to promote the strike as an unmitigated victory. Shaw must have figured that the "victimized American food industry" line had worked so well during the strike, why abandon it when it also would make a very good marketing gimmick. He didn't think he had anything to fear from the local press.

A couple of weeks ago I called Joe to make sure I had the facts right. I told him I wanted to print the story. He checked it out, and now you have it in your hands.

The pictures and Joe's account are proof enough for me. But since these are serious charges I decided to talk to a couple of Shaw workers, to see if they would confirm the story. They did, they were willing to be quoted, but they did not want their names used. Here are their versions. First, from a line worker:

> In early 1986 I heard rumors that during the night at the furthest corner of the plant they had scab crews opening up small boxes of Mexican cauliflower and broccoli and dumping them into totes. About six months after I heard it, I had occasion to go back there between the freezer and the wall — definitely not a work area — and I saw men dumping cauliflower from boxes marked 'product of Mexico' into unmarked bins. Then a forklift driver would come and put the totes into storage with the other Shaw product. The boxes were blue and white, about 40 pounds. There must have been about six men and one forklift driver.
>
> You know in a plant, anything they try to

keep a secret is the first thing you find out about. It was especially suspicious because the work was not being done in a regular work area.

After that, we started using tote bins that were marked 'product of Mexico.' These totes would go right to the head of the line and people could see the mark stamped on the side. People talked, and the explanation that was given was that as long as it didn't go into a bag or a box with a THANKS label on it, it was legal. We run many labels, some of them have THANKS stickers, and some of them don't. I assumed they tried to keep the labels straight.

It is quite a conversation piece. For a while there it was one of the main jokes in the plant.

And here is what a line mechanic had to say:

Some mornings they bring a lot of small boxes marked 'product of Mexico' into the plant, break them open, and pour the cauliflower or broccoli right on the line. I have seen it with my own eyes. I don't know where they bring the boxes from, but I know what it says on the box. They don't hide it. They just do it. Everybody knows it. But people are worried about saying anything to a reporter. The moment you tell someone and give your name, you are going to lose your job.

I worked over at Farmers' a couple of times. There I saw the big totes with 'product of Mexico' stamped on them.

25

One time I made a joke to a lead man. 'Boy, we sure do have a lot of Mexican food in here.' He got serious and said we were not supposed to say anything about that. He was aware of it, just like everybody else. He didn't try to justify it.

That's all folks. The story no longer fits in the file marked, "open secret — known by many — but not reported by press." I have moved it to the category titled, "as charged by a small alternative newspaper." Let's see what happens next.

(September, 1989)

Richard Shaw *(Photo: Kurt Ellison/Register-Pajaronian)*

4

THANKS For The
Memories, Richard

We get letters.

Gentlemen:

This office represents Richard A. Shaw, Inc. and Richard Shaw individually. The purpose of this letter is to advise you that the September 1989 issue of *El Andar* contained an article entitled, "Thanks, But No Thanks" by Frank Bardacke. Said article is libelous per se and is replete with factual inaccuracies and irresponsible journalism.

On behalf of Richard A. Shaw, Inc. and Richard Shaw individually, demand is hereby made upon both El Andar Publications and Frank Bardacke to print a retraction which shall include, but not be limited to, a true statement of the facts.

You have accused my clients of "fraud," "lies," and "gimmicks." In the event that you fail to retract these inflammatory statements and publish the correct facts, I have been authorized to initiate litigation against both Frank Bardacke and El Andar Publications to seek both compensatory and punitive damages.

The formation of the nonprofit organization known as THANKS was clearly intended to encourage the support of American farmers and the purchase of American grown farm products. Richard A. Shaw, Inc. in promoting the THANKS program actively supported the primary policies of THANKS. Richard A. Shaw, Inc. has remained steadfast in its endeavor to buy product from domestic farmers.

The alleged pictures referred to in the September 1989 article were in fact taken in 1988, not in 1987 as the article states.

The purchase of minimal amounts of products from Mexico was necessitated by the fact that local farmers were unable to supply Richard A. Shaw, Inc. with adequate amounts of cauliflower to satisfy customer requirements.

Between April 1986 and October 1988 my client purchased and received less than 1/200 of 1% of their packed product from Mexico. Between October 1986 and October 1989 less than 1% of the total product packed by Richard A. Shaw Inc. was purchased from Mexico. At no time prior to or since the inception of THANKS has my client ever purchased broccoli from Mexico.

Furthermore, although less than 1% of the annual budgeted pack is purchased from Mexico, the same stringent requirements with regard to quality are enforced through both the quality control experts at Richard A. Shaw, Inc. as well as the requirement of meeting all specifications of the United States Food and Drug Administration.

Nothing that has occurred since 1986 violates either the spirit or the intent of the formation of THANKS and it is imperative that both Mr. Bardacke and El Andar Publications rectify this gross misrepresentation, retract the libelous statements and publish the correct facts as set forth above.

Should you have any questions, I will be happy to review this matter at a mutually convenient time and place.

Very truly yours,
HARRY C. COOLIDGE

Yes, Mr. Coolidge. The photos of Shaw workers transferring cauliflower from boxes marked "product of Mexico" into unmarked Shaw company bins were taken on June 17, 1988, not June 17, 1987. How that makes any difference is beyond me.

Here is the main point, once again. While Richard Shaw was waging a campaign against Mexican produce, his own company was secretly buying it in bulk form and repacking it in smaller packages.

One need go no further than Shaw's own propaganda to document this deceit. A THANKS publicity handout distributed to the public and the press in the spring of 1986 contained a reprint of an article by Mitzi Ayala which was published in the April 11, 1986 issue of *From the Farmer to You*. In that THANKS puff piece Ms. Ayala reported that Richard Shaw, the founder of THANKS, said "from 1986 on, he'd only buy

31

from American growers." The handout had a cover letter from Richard Shaw himself. Nowhere in that handout did Shaw deny, or mitigate in any way, his reported pledge not to buy foreign produce. Nor does Mr. Coolidge, in his letter to *El Andar*, now deny that Shaw made such a pledge.

It was only after Shaw was caught packing Mexican cauliflower that he admitted doing it. Now he offers various explanations, which may or may not be true. The excuses are a form of damage control; they came after his secret was out.

So my charge stands. Shaw was lying.

The broccoli question is only a little more complicated. Two Shaw workers told me they saw Mexican broccoli processed in the Shaw plant, just as they, and others, told me Shaw was packing Mexican cauliflower. But I was, and continue to be, unwilling to jeopardize their jobs by revealing their names. Therefore, I did not write the THANKS story until we actually had pictures of the Mexican cauliflower. We do not have pictures of Mexican broccoli. Considering how good Shaw's word proved to be about the cauliflower, I leave it to our readers to decide about the broccoli.

I have little to say about Mr. Coolidge's statistics. I do not have access to the full figures—no one except top people at Shaw do. They can play with the numbers any way they want. Is it not truly remarkable, however, that when Mexican product was only "1/200 of 1%" of Shaw's production, we happened to get pictures of it? With that kind of luck we ought to give up this newspaper business and buy lottery tickets.

I could leave it at that. Hopefully this dispute has clarified the complicated relationship between Mexican and "American" frozen food production: most Mexican frozen food is repacked in the United States and then resold on the domestic market. The rest is old news. Shaw has retired, sold his company to the big money boys from Chicago, the transnational food conglomerate, Dean Foods. THANKS as an effective marketing scheme, or "gimmick" if you will, Counselor Coolidge, is long gone. The THANKS bumper stickers, which you could once buy for $1 at the Shaw plant, now sell for just a quarter.

But Mr. Coolidge's letter requires another kind of response. It is not so much an announcement of an impending lawsuit, as it is a threat, an attempt to intimidate *El Andar* and shut me up. "Winning through intimidation," is a main chapter in Richard Shaw's *Book of Success*, as most everyone knows who ever worked in the Richard Shaw plant. Here I do not depend on the word of others, as I spent some time there myself between 1979 and 1981 loading trucks for General Produce. Foremen at Shaw were typically large men, a threatening presence among the workforce; floorladies ruled through a combination of insult and favoritism. When I was there, the loading dock was ruled by Dave Shaw, Dick's brother, who screamed and yelled his way through most days. On one occasion I saw him (with my own eyes, Your Honor) grab a forklift driver—a full head shorter and some forty pounds lighter than he —and shake him back and forth while shouting violently in his face about some supposed error.

And if that doesn't give you a flavor for how these guys operate, try this. Teamster Local 912 veteran John Bubich first told me this story of Dick Shaw's early career when we worked on the line together at H&H Bottling. Anyone who wants to verify Brother Bubich's account can check the May, 1950 issues of the *Register-Pajaronian,* available at the Watsonville Library. (If you go over there on a weekday afternoon you might talk to Bubich himself, a great story teller who can fill you in on a few more Dick Shaw gems.) In the 1950 frozen food workers' strike, a long battle which prepared the ground for the establishment of Teamster Local 912, Richard Shaw was a foreman at one of the struck plants, Fresh Frozen Foods. One of his jobs was to bring strikebreakers through the picket line and into the plant. During a picket line scuffle among four women (two strikers and two strikebreakers), Bubich and several others saw Shaw come out of the plant brandishing a shotgun. He pointed the gun at the unarmed pickets and threatened to use it. The loaded gun was later confiscated from another person inside the struck plant. Police Chief Frank Osmer (Dennis's dad) refused to press charges "because the shotgun had been held on private property." At a later trial of two of the women involved (can you guess which ones were arrested—the strikers or the scabs?) some witnesses agreed that Shaw had carried the shotgun, while others said he carried only a length of pipe.

If I were to leave you with one lasting picture of the career of Richard Shaw, it would not be that he was caught in a stupid lie. That is a human enough error—something that has happened to many of us. Nor would it be that his brother used to run the Shaw loading dock like some sort of feudal fiefdom. Nor even that Dick as a young man threatened un-armed pickets with a shotgun. Rather it would be the follow-ing story, told to me by Joe Fahey, current president of Local 912, who was quick-witted enough to get the pictures which started this whole business. It seems that in May of 1988 (I hope we have the dates right this time) Shaw management decided that too many women were going to the bathroom on company time. It is the legal right of any worker to go to the bathroom when she or he feels it is necessary. Shaw, however, wanted to force his line workers to wait until their formal ten-minute break time. That might mean a wait of up to two hours. As a way of imposing this illegal rule, Shaw Inc. actually placed a floorlady at the bathroom — with clipboard and stop watch — whose job it was to take the names of the women who were in the toilet and how much time they spent there.

The Shaw Toilet Campaign was defeated when 85 women lined up to go to the bathroom during their ten-minute break, not returning to work on the line until they were done.

Richard Shaw is a regular One-Eyed Jack in this town: from frozen food mechanic to owner of his own plant; Watsonville Man of the Year and Salvation Army bell ringer. But now you can see the other side of his face; he is a small town bully. Just as he tried to bully his workers out of their right to go to the bathroom, he now uses his mouthpiece to try to bully us out of our right to tell our view of his dirty public history. He failed inside the plant, and he has failed here.

(December 1989)

Editor's note: Mr. Coolidge never again contacted Frank Bardacke or El Andar.

Grand Metropolitan CEO Allan Sheppard and Finance Director David Nash in London before the news conference where they announced that in 1990 Grand Met's profits increased more than 25 percent to 1.7 billion dollars *(Photo: Peter Trievnor, London Times)*

5

The End of "Think Globally, Act Locally"?

THINK GLOBALLY: The layoff of nearly 400 people at our local Green Giant plant is a result of three major trends in world capitalism: Third World debt, internationalization of the food supply; and leveraged buyouts.

These are complicated and interrelated phenomena, and they are most easily discussed one at a time.

• **Third World debt.** In the late 1970s, U.S. banks made "development" loans to Third World governments. These loans came to grief, as even supposedly solvent countries like Brazil and Mexico were unable to repay them. As a way of avoiding a complete loss, bank consortiums such as the International Monetary Fund and World Bank arranged for further loans with new conditions. These new loans obligated the debtor countries to cut government spending, open up their economies even further to North American capital, and enlarge their exports. International financiers designed such policies so that Third World countries could earn more dollars and repay the banks.

Thus, Mexico converted much of its agricultural heartland, *El Bajío*, which used to produce corn and beans for domestic consumption, as well as sisal for export, into land for the production of broccoli and cauliflower for export. The Mexicans, the first people in the world to cultivate corn, are now forced to import it. This, coupled with the reduction of government subsidies on corn meal, raised the price of tortillas several hundred percent.

• **Internationalization of the food supply**. Fresh fruits and vegetables, grown in far-off places like New Zealand, Chile, and North Africa, are now flown to U.S. cities and made available to consumers in the dead of winter. When even moderately prosperous people began to eat fresh vegetables year 'round, the frozen vegetable market stagnated. Hurt by a slump in sales, transnational frozen food companies, first Birds Eye and then Green Giant, moved some production of bulk frozen food to Mexico and Guatemala in search of lower wages and production costs.

• **Leveraged buyouts**. Starting in the 1980s, some corporations borrowed large amounts of money, not for investment in productive enterprise, but rather to take over other corporations. They then needed to ruthlessly cut costs so that they could repay the debt they incurred in the takeovers.

Thus, in 1988 Grand Metropolitan, centered in London, maneuvered a leveraged buyout of Pillsbury (which had earlier bought out Green Giant). Soon thereafter they fired 500 Pillsbury middle-management types, and, finally, to get to the punch line, decided to gut their Watsonville operation. The jobs of the Watsonville workers will now be done by Mexican workers earning about four dollars a day, or by workers in Ohio earning close to minimum wage.

Let's put this in plain language. So that New York bankers will get paid in full on some bad loans they made, so that frozen food executives will make super profits rather than ordinary ones, and so that the Grand Metropolitan board of directors can win its financial gamble and make the payments on its high interest loans, impoverished Mexican mothers no longer can afford to buy enough tortillas for their hungry children, and unemployed Watsonville frozen food workers don't know how they are going to pay their rent.

ACT LOCALLY: Have we reached the limits of this popular Santa Cruz County political slogan? How can local action influence world-wide market trends or change policies of the IMF and World Bank, or affect the decisions of the board of directors of the multi-billion dollar Grand Met? Isn't this an issue out of our control, where we have no other choice than to suffer through it, making do as best we can?

That is obviously the opinion of recognized cannery worker leaders. Oscar Rios, Cannery Worker Project Director, complained to his fellow city council members about the "greed" of Grand Met, but offered us no way to fight the layoffs. Taking another tack, Teamster chief Sergio Lopez promised the *Register-Pajaronian* that the union is "actively working on things that will be of great interest," but was unable to say what those things might be.

Perhaps these people are right, and nothing can be done. But institutionalized leaders rarely initiate struggles themselves, especially when the odds are heavily against winning. The people who are willing to risk fighting and losing are people with little to lose.

In this case that means the soon to be laid off Green Giant workers. What are they willing to do? If enough of them were determined to act, that in itself would change the political situation, and perhaps make some kind of winning strategy possible.

A few weeks ago I saw a play about the Green Giant layoffs put on by a Cabrillo College English as a Second Language class in the La Manzana courtyard. The play was written and produced by Cabrillo students, some of whom work at Green Giant, and most of whom are local agricultural workers.

A melodramatic story of the layoffs, the play concludes with the death of the wife of a Green Giant worker. Ill before the layoff announcement, she dies from grief and worry when she learns of her husband's impending unemployment.

Her last words are straight from Joe Hill, "Don't mourn, organize," and the curtain falls with the whole cast on stage singing a Spanish version of "We Shall Not Be Moved."

The whole point of the play is "We Must Do Something," although it never suggests what that something might be. Afterwards several people who work at Green Giant stayed around and talked. Yes, they want to fight the layoffs, but don't know how to do it.

Well, what can we do?

Any local action must reach out to other communities and seek the support of people who might have their own grievances with Grand Met, the IMF and the World Bank. In this situation, "An injury to one is an injury to all" (the old Industrial Workers of the World slogan) is a more useful guide than "Think globally, act locally."

Over the last several years, boycotts — and the threat of boycotts — have been the main weapon of workers trying to reach out to potential allies. At times the UFW has used the boycott effectively; GM workers in Van Nuys managed for a time to keep their plant open with the threat of a Southern California boycott of GM cars; and even here in Watsonville, the Wells Fargo boycott was partially responsible for forcing the end of the Watsonville frozen food strike.

Why not a boycott of Burger King and other Grand Met companies? Grand Met spends millions of dollars establishing brand recognition; we can do our best to give those brands a bad name. Here is just a short list of what Grand Met owns and sells: Popov and Smirnoff Vodka, Gilby's Gin, J&B Scotch, as well as 14 other brands of alcohol; Alpo Dog food; Pearle Health Services ("the largest retailer of eye care products in the world," brags the Grand Met 1988 annual report); Ski Yogurt; Haagen Daz Ice Cream; and Burger King.

I pick Burger King as the main target of the boycott for several reasons. It is already under fire from environmental groups because the beef for their burgers comes from cows that are grazing on what used to be Central American rain forests. Burger King is a cheap fast-food place where working class people eat, and it is among such people that we will find our strongest allies. Burger King is already in trouble, and Grand Met has spent a lot money trying to increase its sales. And lastly, it is a boycott that we can start right here in Watsonville on Freedom Boulevard.

Will you dream along with me? A small group of Watsonville Green Giant workers starts a boycott of the Freedom Boulevard Burger King, demanding that all local Green Giant layoffs be rescinded. The boycott is tremendously successful as the whole community responds. Acknowledged "cannery worker leaders" endorse the boycott and it spreads throughout Santa Cruz County. The national Chicano movement takes it up (as they did the Coors boycott) and declares the eating of a Burger King hamburger a betrayal of the Chicano and Mexican people. Laid off Green Giant workers in Fridley, Minnesota, and Terre Haute, Indiana, endorse the boycott, making it a national event. Unable to ignore the movement any longer, the Teamsters Union joins in and puts all Grand Met products on its Don't Buy list. Finally, the boycott is endorsed by all major environmental groups, as part of their effort to protect the world's rain forests. Burger King profits fall sharply...and negotiations begin.

Sure it's a dream. But if a group of workers at Green Giant want to make that dream come true, and are willing to work for it, they have a chance. I, for one, hope they give it a try.

(June, 1990)

Martin Luther King Day, 1992 *(Photo: Kurt Ellison/Register-Pajaronian)*

6

MLK's Birthday: Listen to the Music

I read in the newspaper that George Bush went to Atlanta on Martin Luther King's birthday to join hands with Coretta King and sing "We Shall Overcome." Terrific. That deadly anthem was never a favorite of mine, with its plaintive, suffering moan about what we might do "someday." George Bush can have it.

Some songs from the Civil Rights movement he will never sing: upbeat, humorous, picket line songs.

If you miss me on the picket line
and you can't find me nowhere
oh, oh, oh,
come on over to the city jail
I'll be rooming up there...

Mississippi River, cotton fields, colored schools, the back of the bus, the song goes on and on about places people might be missed. I fear the words can not convey the feeling, and reading and writing being what they are, I can not sing them to you from inside these pages. But it is no surprise that McDonald's didn't use this song for its candle-lit commercial which seems to celebrate King's death as much as his birth.

On the day designated to celebrate MLK's birthday—
what an outrage to tradition and history, this practice of
celebrating birthdays so they make a three-day weekend—the
displaced Green Giant workers called for a demonstration in
honor of King and to mark the one-year anniversary of the
Green Giant layoffs. No more than 50 of us answered the call,
and seeing us from a passing car as we stood in front of the
Green Giant gates, we must have seemed a pitiful few.

But, as the song goes, "listen to the music." On the march
from what remains of San Patricio to what remains of Green
Giant (down Ford to Rodriguez, left on Rodriguez to Beach),
a small group of people, accompanied by guitar, sang from a
Catholic Choir songbook, *Flor y Canto*. No obnoxious leader
armed with a hand-held megaphone urged us to sing along; no
jerks in armbands made sure we stayed in line. Rather we
strolled leisurely, under a blue winter sky, chatting and listen-
ing to the melodious songs of popular struggle.

Hay que ser atrevidos
y decididos a dar la vida
tomen sus decisiones
tomen sus decisiones y consecuencias
y consecuencias...

Alicia Martinez, a member of San Patricio's Sunday
Choir, mother of three who works at night cleaning banks, was
the lead singer, urging us to be bold and daring. But plenty of
others knew the song and joined in.

The speeches at the gate reflected the mood of the crowd,
which continued to be upbeat after the short march. About a
third of the marchers entertained the rest of us with a warm
spirited skit about the dangers of NAFTA. Bob Gomez, the
local migrant education resource teacher and musician
extraordinaire, read a poem about his dream for Watsonville,

and sang two satirical songs. The last one, "*De Cabrones,*" we sang to the tune of "*De Colores*" and finished with these lines:

...y quisiera cortar los cojones
de muchos cabrones que frustan a mi.

Well, maybe you had to be there. But the good cheer which marked the day was not forced; the group of 20 displaced Green Giant workers at the heart of the demonstration have a lot to be proud of. They have been fighting, against overwhelming odds, ever since Grand Metropolitan, in January of 1990, announced it was going to fire two-thirds of its Watsonville workers and move production to Irapuato, Mexico. It was these people, mostly middle-aged Mexican women, who first fingered the true villains of the story, the board of directors of Grand Met. It was they who fought against the racism and bureaucratic nonsense in the laid off worker retraining program. It was their struggle which forced Grand Met to admit that it is polluting Irapuato's water supply. And it is their continuing boycott, with picket lines here in Watsonville and literature distributed around the world, which helps give depth to the continent-wide struggle against the Free Trade Agreement.

The people who rule this country started rewriting the story of Martin Luther King on the night of his assassination, and we can expect that American presidents will continue to mouth the words of "We Shall Overcome" as long as there are TV cameras willing to film them. Martin Luther King is valuable to them because he preached non-violence to the oppressed. For us, though we may have had some tactical differences with him along the way, he will always be a stubborn, unbelievably eloquent, champion of justice. Can anyone deny that if the Most Reverend Doctor Junior had been in Watsonville on January 20, 1992, the numbers on our march would have increased by at least one?

(February, 1992)

47

Land

Irrigators laying pipe *(Photo: Kurt Ellison/Register-Pajaronian)*

7

The Franich Annexation

In 1983 my old dog, Moss, died. He was weak and infirm by then, not even able to accompany me on his favorite morning walk for a newspaper two blocks down Prospect Street to Dick's Liquors. He mostly just lay around the house, sleeping and scratching; his bad smell dominated whatever room he was in, and he was becoming a burden even to those of us who had hand fed him as a pup, twelve years before.

He died in the afternoon, soon after I came home from work. He was lying in one of his favorite spots in the front room. I gave him a little push in the hindquarters.

"Hey Moss."

His body was rigid under my hand, but he turned his head and tossed me one last look through glazed eyes, and then his jaw slumped to the floor.

Now what? He was a big dog, born in Moss Landing to a Shepherd-Lab mix and supposedly fathered by a Great Dane. He was too big to bury in my back yard. Why not take him to the apple orchard just east of the East Lake Shopping Center? We had walked through it together many times when he was younger, and if he were buried there I could throw him a thought every time I drove by on my way to the Fairgrounds or up Hecker Pass.

I wrapped him in an old blanket and lugged him into the station wagon. Blood ran out his ass onto the floor, front steps, and sidewalk. In a few minutes I was in the orchard. I backed the wagon under an old tree, dug a shallow grave, pushed him into it face down, and shoveled the dirt back over him. I tried to level the earth, but I couldn't help leaving a mound—a cliched image of a grave. I carved his name and dates on the tree and left.

I had just buried my dog in what has become the crucial political issue in the Pajaro Valley: the proposed Franich Annexation.

Tony Franich's attempt to annex his 78-acre apple orchard to the City of Watsonville so that it can be sold for housing development has finally put the question before us: will Watsonville continue to be a relatively prosperous working class community where people live and work in town, or will it become a bedroom for San Jose, with expensive suburban housing sitting next to a growing Mexican slum?

The Franich orchard sits on the eastern side of the valley corridor extending from Mt. Madonna to the sea. It is prime agricultural land, the best we have. It is this land that the county government is mandated by state law to protect, with a majority of the county supervisors having the political inclination to follow that mandate. Franich wants to make an end run around those officials by annexing the land to the city so that a development-crazed city council will permit him to sell the land for housing.

What's in it for him? The difference between $18,000 an acre if the land can be used only for agriculture, and $110,000 an acre if the land can be used for houses.

Why such an enormous difference in price? Because we sit so close to the expanding electronics industry, slowly moving south from San Jose. Just ten years ago Watsonville sat at the head of the Salinas Valley, facing south. Our main connection to the world was through Prunedale by way of San Miguel Pass, and through Castroville by way of old Highway 1, into the fields of Salinas. Truck after truck of broccoli, cauliflower, spinach, and other vegetables traveled those roads into our frozen food plants.

That travel has not diminished by much; nevertheless Watsonville nearly has been overwhelmed by the new traffic north. Computer production has crept over Highway 17 into Scotts Valley, and in the last ten years housing projects have shot up on the north side of town, peopled by folks who come to Watsonville to sleep by the Pacific Ocean, leaving low paid computer assembly line workers to live in the smog and drink the polluted water of what was once the Santa Clara Valley. We now seem to sit, not at the head of the Salinas Valley, but at the foot of the Valley of Silicon.

Tony Franich walks around town in beat up old clothes, pretending to be a farmer. But he is really just a businessman, unwilling to farm at a small profit year after year, because he can get an immediate big profit by paving over his land and dividing it up for houses. But once the houses are built, the land will not generate any more wealth. The real estate interests will have made a "killing" in more ways than one. The basis on which our prosperous little farm town was built — rich, rich topsoil, warmed by the California sun and cooled by the coastal fog, will be gone. And that is why Franich's sale is the first official step in Watsonville becoming a bedroom community and a Mexican slum. Once the land is paved over, where are people going to work?

That question was in the mind of Francisco Juarez of the Watsonville UFW local, who argued against the Franich Annexation at a recent forum, saying it will mean the loss of

200 jobs. This opposition by local workers to a development scheme has a significance far beyond Watsonville. Since "preserving the environment" became an issue in the early 1970s, workers usually have been pro-development, arguing that saving the environment cost them jobs. But from the Amazon forests of Brazil, to the redwoods of the North Coast, to the fishing bays of Alaska, workers are now beginning to see that they have an interest in "environmentalism."

If development is allowed to follow the highest rate of profit all over the globe, eventually there won't be any jobs for anyone. How can the rubber tappers of the Amazon make a living if their forests are destroyed? Or the lumberjacks of Humboldt County once the old growth is clear-cut? Or the fishermen of Alaska, once the oil companies have destroyed their waters? And now we can add Watsonville to the list. How will the farm workers and cannery workers make a living once the farm land is paved over?

None of this seems to matter to Squire Franich. According to him, the orchard is his land and he should be able to do whatever he wants with it. When the Santa Cruz County Local Agency Formation Commission (LAFCO) blocked his attempt to put the land under the authority of the Watsonville City Council, he went to Sacramento and tried to buy himself a law that would allow the transfer. Given what he stood to gain, the California Legislature came cheap. For $26,000 he put the bill in motion. Unfortunately for him, during the process the FBI started indicting state legislators for just these kinds of shenanigans and Franich's buddy, liberal Henry Mello, couldn't manage to get the bill passed.

Franich's shameless opportunism is best seen in that little "26 grand donation." Three thousand dollars of it went to Willie Brown. Do you know what Franich must think of black liberal Democrat Willie Brown? Maybe this will give you a hint. Franich was one of a crowd of right-wingers who paid $50 a seat to hear and support Ollie North when he spoke at the Doubletree Inn in Monterey in May of 1988. When a demonstrator got up during the speech and ran down the aisle shouting, "Ollie North behind bars, throw the bum in jail," he was jumped and subdued by Monterey County sheriffs. Once the young man was under control the voice of farmer Franich was heard to cry out, "Kill the sonofabitch, kill the sonofabitch!"

A serious battle is shaping up. Can a coalition of agricultural workers who want to save their jobs, local residents who want to protect Watsonville as a small farming community, and liberal county officials successfully beat back local agribusiness and real estate interests who are doing what you are supposed to do in a capitalist economy — go for the highest rate of profit? Probably not. If the future of our valley hangs on the difference between the price of a silicon chip and the price of a flat of strawberries, our main hope is that the computer industry will bust sooner rather than later.

But we need not be total victims of market forces. A strong enough movement, backed by state law, could save the valley. Rumors abound that LAFCO is going to hold its next hearing on the proposed annexation at night in Watsonville (rather than during the day in Santa Cruz). The county officials are hoping a strong community turnout will support them in a decision to stop the annexation. See you there.

I have plenty of Moss stories. The time in Salinas when I mistakenly left him at a used car lot, and he ran across town seeking refuge at a house of a friend of mine, where he had been only a few times before....the time he jumped out of the back of my truck to chase a cat across the street and ran smack into a VW bug, denting the fender and stopping the car, but barely slowing down himself....and, well, I could easily bore you with dog stories. But Moss's last story — what a surprise.

By the time he died Moss was already too big for my part of town. Too many houses, too many cars, he was a bit of a nuisance to the neighborhood. Now he lies buried in a piece of land whose fate promises to tell us what kind of future Watsonville might have. A future where we still have some farm dogs running free, who die with enough open space to be buried beneath their owners' feet. Or a future filled with leashed lap dogs, whose owners must follow them around with bags and sticks to clean their doo-doo off the sidewalks. Dogs, who when they die, are picked up by young men from the Correct Agency, who dispose of them, safely out of sight.

(July, 1989)

(Photo: Jon Silver)

8

Airport Conversion: Will It Fly?

When I was growing up my father had a standard remark for a certain kind of impossible situation: "If we had some ham, we could have some ham and eggs, if we had some eggs." I can't think of a better way to sum up the Watsonville housing crisis.

According to official city figures, right now we need 2,585 more housing units for low-income households. At the current growth rate of 200 units per year, it would take us about 13 years to build enough houses just to meet current needs. And that assumes that every new house would be "affordable," an impossibility given the cost of Pajaro Valley land.

What land? Where could we put these fictitious houses? There is not enough land within the city limits to build even half of these units. If we expand the city, and build on newly annexed outlying areas, we destroy the ecological and economic basis of our community — prime agricultural land.

Not enough houses and nowhere to put them. Neither ham, nor eggs.

So I wonder what our mayor meant when he told the Watsonville Rotary Club that "we can deal with the housing crisis without scrapping the airport." I missed that particular luncheon, and the *Register-Pajaronian* did not give the details of any proposed plan Mayor McFarren might have. We need specifics, Mr. Mayor, specifics. Do you have an actual, concrete plan, or just a vague hope that perhaps, somehow, a plan will emerge?

Unless we can acquire a large amount of cheap land, there is no solution to the housing crisis. Rent control is important to hold down the cost of the housing we have now, and a strong inclusionary ordinance will force the developers to build us a few hundred low-cost units. But without cheap land, it is impossible to build enough low-cost houses.

And where is there any cheap land around here? The only answer I know of is the 290 acres of the Watsonville Municipal Airport. Those acres, already owned by the city, could be transferred or sold to a non-profit housing agency, potential residents, or even developers. On that land we could build a model housing project: low and moderate-income housing units, settled among a group of large and small parks. Throw in a few new schools, and we would still have enough room for a pleasant little aviation museum.

But the small number of people who currently use the airport do not want a museum. They want their airport. And they are using all sorts of arguments to defend it. I spent a large part of the last few months trying to check out their claims, and here is what I learned.

FALSE CLAIM #1: The Navy gave the airport to Watsonville, and the federal government has a veto over whatever happens to airport land.

AS IT TURNS OUT: In 1942 after a bond election, the city of Watsonville bought more than 285 acres of land for the airport. The land was then leased to the Federal Aviation Authority for $1, the lease to end six months after the end of W.W.II. The federal government built the runways and airport buildings. After the war, the Feds returned the land to the city, and transferred (for $1) about 20 acres of it to the Freedom School District. Some of the old airport buildings were used for the first Freedom Elementary School. Later, the school was moved, and the part of the airport between Roach Road and Freedom Boulevard was sold to a San Jose developer.

This use of old airport buildings for a school sets a clear precedent, as does the sale of some airport land. The airport belongs to the city of Watsonville; what happens to it is a matter of public policy. Once Watsonville decides what is the best use of the land, then we can negotiate with other concerned governmental bodies — county, state, and federal. Conversion of the airport is not illegal.

FALSE CLAIM #2: The airport is needed for emergencies.

AS IT TURNS OUT: Highway 1, Routes 129, and 152, and San Miguel Canyon Pass give us freeway access. In an emergency, small planes could land on one of the many private airstrips in the area. Watsonville Hospital has a helio-pad.

FALSE CLAIM #3: The airport does a significant amount of commercial business, and shutting it down will hurt the local economy.

AS IT TURNS OUT: Claims that the airport plays a large role in the local economy were hard to check out. At various times I heard or read that the airport was used to ship flowers or produce, as well as being a major distribution center for UPS and Federal Express. I wrote a letter to Airport Manager Kimberly Wirht, specifically asking her what commercial cargo flew in or out of the airport. In a follow-up interview, Ms. Wirht was polite but uncooperative. While assuring me that the airport was crucial to local business, she could give me no specifics. I would have to wait, she said, until the Association of Monterey Bay Area Governments (AMBAG) completes their local transportation study.

I took that at face value. While I couldn't quite fathom where AMBAG was going to get their figures about the Watsonville airport if not from Ms. Wirht herself, I could understand her reluctance to drop everything and provide me with specific information.

But now that I have looked into the issue more thoroughly, I believe Ms. Wirht could not give me specific numbers because there are no numbers. Virtually no commercial cargo moves through the Watsonville Municipal Airport. No flowers fly out; they are trucked to San Jose or San Francisco and flown from there. It is the same with berries and all other agricultural produce. Federal Express, which Ms. Wirht told the *Santa Cruz Sentinel* was one of the many commercial users of the airport, flies none of its business out of Watsonville. It is all trucked over Highway 17 to the San Jose International Airport.

After workers at Federal Express told me this, I looked back at my notes of the interview with Ms. Wirht. Sure enough, she said Federal Express was a local user of the airport. Quite a neat technique. You make a general claim that the airport is commercially important, making reference to some companies that use it. Then when someone asks you for specific numbers, you say you have none. And, in fact, some of what you said is false. What gives Ms. Wirht?

The only commercial cargo that I could verify moving in or out of Watsonville is the daily flight by UPS. And according to local union officials, UPS plans to consolidate all its Santa Cruz County business in one Santa Cruz city office, and is going to close down its Watsonville operation, Watsonville airport or not.

It may be that there is some other commercial cargo that I missed—but I tracked down every claim I heard. And only UPS turned out to be true. (Local drug dealers are as reluctant as Ms. Wirht to provide specific information.)

But when people talk about the commercial importance of the airport, often they don't mean cargo. What they are talking about are executive flights. The favorite example is Granite Construction.

The argument goes something like this. Granite Construction has its main corporate offices here in Watsonville, although it operates all over the West. If we close down the airport, and deny executives the convenience of an airplane five minutes away from their corporate desks, maybe they will move out of Watsonville, and take about 60 local jobs with them.

I must admit the argument stops me cold. I don't think Granite would move out of town just because their executives have to drive a half hour to the Salinas or Monterey airports. Bul I can't be sure. If the real reason the airport is necessary, however, is for the convenience of a handful of executives, I have a couple of suggestions. First, let's make one of the executives explain, face to face, to a Watsonville family living in a garage that the airport land can not be used for new housing, because on those occasions when he flies, he prefers a five-minute drive to a thirty-minute one.

Second, as a practical solution to this problem, I suggest that in exchange for using the airport land for housing, the city provide limousine or helicopter service between Watsonville and the Salinas airport, for all local executives. Acquiring land for low-cost housing would be well worth the cost of such service.

Do you think people defending the airport will accept this last offer? No way. Even the argument about executive use is beside the point, and designed to hide the bald truth: The Watsonville Municipal Airport is primarily a recreational facility. It is a toy for the rich; an airplane theme park for adults.

Opposition to airport conversion is led by the local Aircraft Owners and Pilots Association. But uneasiness about closing the airport is much more widespread than that. Many well-meaning people, who have no direct connection to the local airport, oppose shutting it down. Their opposition is based on some kind of civic pride, a belief that closing the airport would be a step backward for Watsonville.

This argument is difficult to deal with, because it is a vague feeling, rather than an articulated position. And civic pride is good, something to be encouraged. I would ask of these people the following: wouldn't they feel even prouder of Watsonville if we could actually house all our people? Doesn't it make them feel ashamed that so many people in our community live in terrible conditions? Imagine the pride we would feel if we created a model housing development that would be an example to other cities across the United States? Wouldn't that be more important than an airport?

Winning this debate is not going to win us the airport land. We can pile compelling argument on top of compelling argument, with little effect. It is a question of political power. The Pilots Association has lots. The real estate industry—which does not want low-cost housing at all—has even more. The few executives who do use the airport are some of the most influential people in town.

To defeat this coalition would take a great effort. We would have to mobilize great numbers of people, over a long period of time. But it can be done. The Scotts Valley airport was closed down. People in Riverside County shut down the Tri-City Airport. Small communities across the country are considering whether or not they can afford local airports.

Over the last decade the people of Watsonville have won some extraordinary political battles. We fought the *Migra* to a standstill. We waged one of the strongest strikes in recent

American history. We came back from the devastation of the earthquake, and managed to get hundreds of trailers from FEMA. We won the struggle for district elections, and then elected a left/liberal city council to replace a conservative regime that had run the city since the 1950s. Are we strong enough now to shut down the airport and use the land for the benefit of the whole community?

(May, 1990)

Strawberries under plastic *(Photo: Jon Silver)*

9

Not Enough Water
to Wash Their Sins Away

Imported water, argues Ivan Illich in his book, *H2O and the Waters of Forgetfulness,* converted Rome from a city to an Empire. Two hundred and fifty miles of aqueducts brought mountain streams to city fountains, pierced city walls, and destroyed the magic circle that separated Rome's inside from its outside. Free from its dependence on the Tiber, some springs, and a few wells, Rome exploded from within. A million people, each using 100 gallons of water a year, sprawled from city to suburb. To be a citizen of Rome no longer located a person in a particular geographical place. Florence, Naples, Gaul, Iberia — if it were all Roman, what was Rome? The Empire was built and the city was lost.

Imported water will not transform Watsonville into an Empire. But it will fully integrate us into the Hydraulic Empire of the American West. And it will destroy the Pajaro Valley as a place.

We are already well down that road. Our frozen food industry is owned by two giant transnational corporations, run from London and Chicago. Large corporate conglomerates — Castle & Cooke, Tellis Ranch, the University of California — increasingly dominate decisions about how we farm our fields. We produce according to the dictates of the international market.

Once we decide that we can not live within our limits of earth, air, and water, once we decide to literally plug ourselves into the dams, pumps, aqueducts, and pipes which move the water of the Sierra Nevada some 3,000 miles up and down and sideways across California, then the Pajaro Valley will become a cog, a unit, an element in a giant matrix of inputs and outputs where everything is decided by expert calculus of the bottom line. Imported water will take us to our final destination: we will become a no place.

Arguing against imported water, I do not invoke the dream of an independent Pajaro Valley peopled by the spiritual sons and daughters of the Ohlone, unconnected to the rest of the world. Such a place, in its current romanticized form, never existed. And it is surely not coming back. Nor do I argue that we must cut ourselves off from the world economy in order to survive as a place. Since the early arrival of Europeans and the harvesting of sea otter pelts, cowhides, tallow, and wheat for Europe and Asia, we have been tied to a world market.

What is different now might be seen as merely a matter of scale; imported water would integrate us more fully into the international division of labor and resources. But there comes a time when quantity becomes quality. The Pajaro Valley Water Management Agency (PVWMA) is proposing that we ignore the limits put by local water on local life — that we treat water as a commodity that can never run dry, always to be replenished with money and technique. That in the words of their own brochure the "Agency [should] adopt and implement plans that would decrease present water use rates, and *create* new sources of water" (my italics).

"Create"? A slip of the word processor? No. The word signals Watsonville's belated entry into modern madness where technicians make promises traditionally reserved for the gods.

Enough of that. Let's get to the details. Armed with these ideas about imported water, that's just what I tried to do. Here is what I found out.

Salt water intrusion. By now, you must have heard about it. On a strip of heavily-farmed land, from the mouth of the Salinas River to the fields along San Andreas Road, wells are coming up salty. Near Castroville, where the situation is most severe and where salty wells were first noticed in the early 1940s, wells have been capped and land taken out of production. But what is happening today in Castroville could happen elsewhere tomorrow. Agribusinessmen throughout the Salinas and Pajaro valleys are worried.

Salt water intrusion is not hard to understand. Underground water, like surface water, moves toward the sea. It moves slowly (about two feet a year under the Pajaro Valley, one hydrologist told me) because it is embedded in rock and sand; but its inevitable destination is the great submarine canyon of the Monterey Bay — when all goes well. But what has been "inevitable" since Pleistocene times (about two million years ago) has now become problematic. So much water has been pumped and the level of the water table so reduced, that, rather than fresh water flowing into the sea, the sea is "intruding" into fresh water.

Even without over-pumping, some of this would happen during our dry summer seasons, but in recent years the saline content of coastal wells has not abated even in winter. For almost twenty years now, hydrologists and agricultural technicians have known we have a problem.

The problem is usually blamed on agriculture, which accounts for about 75 percent of the pumping in the Pajaro Valley. But agriculture is too broad a term; market-driven, corporate dominated, agribusiness is a more accurate way to describe the culprit.

What does this mean? Look at the question of crop mix. Since the 1950s, international prices have made row crops — especially strawberries — more profitable than apples. (People can still make money in apples, but not as much as they can make in berries and other row crops.) Thus, in Santa Cruz County, apple orchard acreage has fallen from over 10,000 in 1950 to less than 4,000 today. Apple orchards use one-half as much water as strawberries; our current crop mix is sucking up our water. If agribusinessmen were to consider the effects of their farming practices on the underground water supply, if their decisions were based on anything other than the highest rate of profit, then our valley might still be graced by apple orchards, and our underground water would still flow to the sea.

Don't blame agriculture. This valley could be farmed in a way that would use but not mine underground water. The most obvious solution to salt water intrusion is to suspend farming on the low, sandy soils along the coast, and stop the overpumping required by such farming. Hydrologists, who frequently disagree, do not disagree about that. But that land is privately-owned and corporately-farmed. The PVWMA, which has enough trouble just getting people to register their wells, is not going to tell the Doblers, Capuros, Manfres, Siris, Coastal Berries, and the Tellis Corporation how to farm. No. Instead, they are going to try to import water 71 miles from the San Luis Dam to the Pacific's edge, so that these same people can continue their unreasonable—but highly profitable—agricultural practices.

But in the actually existing (capitalist) world, things are not generally understood as simultaneously "unreasonable" and "highly profitable." We can not expect businessmen, some of whose pesticide-poisoned workers live in caves, to treat our water as anything more than just another commodity. In the real Pajaro Valley, dominated by corporate agriculture, are there some solutions — other than imported water — for salt water intrusion along the coast?

Think little, think small. Think of College Lake. It holds about 3,000 acre-feet of water when allowed to fill — which hardly ever happens. Instead, depending on how wet the year, about 10,000 acre-feet of water is pumped into Salsipuedes Creek, at the north end of the levee where East Lake Avenue and Holohan Road cross. From there it makes its way to the Pajaro River and then out to sea. Some minor work around this natural lake would increase its capacity, protect neighboring lands from flooding, and allow us to use the water (currently being released into the sea) for irrigation. Rather than bringing water from the Sierras, by way of San Luis Dam, to the edge of Pajaro Dunes, why not bring it just eight miles from College Lake?

Think medium. In 1978, cold storage owner Charles Buchwald suggested to the Pajaro Valley Chamber of Commerce and Agriculture that the waste water from the local frozen food industry — which is not as contaminated as other sewage water — be transported to the coast and injected into the ground water supply. A series of "injection wells" along the coast line would dilute the salt in the water and create a water barrier to further sea water intrusion.

Think reclamation. If we must think large, think reclamation, not importation. Current plans to combat sea water intrusion in the neighboring Salinas Valley focus on tertiary treatment of waste water, and then the use of that water to replace coastal pumps in the irrigation of Castroville artichoke fields. Tertiary treated sewage water is being injected into underground water supplies in Fullerton and Irvine. If we upgrade our local sewage plant to do a better job of cleaning waste water (tertiary treatment), we could use that water to irrigate the coastal fields in the summer and for injection wells along the coast in the winter. This is an expensive plan, but still cheaper than imported water.

If reclamation is possible and cheaper, why is agribusiness so enthusiastic about importing water? In thinking about Pajaro Valley politics, we must never forget that while most of the people who own our agricultural land may be farmers in the morning, they think like real estate agents after lunch. They know full well that while lands zoned only for agriculture may sell for as low as $10,000 an acre, that same land zoned for housing can go over $300,000 an acre.* They may want to continue farming now, but they do not want to do anything that might reduce their chances to subdivide in the future.

That's why they prefer imported water. Imported water would be suitable for drinking, while reclaimed water could be used only for irrigation or injection into the ground. In the coming debate between imported and reclaimed water (if the

---

*This 1992 price, gleaned from Watsonville Real Estate listings, is almost three times the 1989 price as reported by the *Register-Pajaronian,* and cited earlier in "The Franich Annexation." What buyers are actually paying, I do not know. But the lot next to my house, one-seventh of an acre in a working class area, just sold for $95,000.

These exaggerated prices, as I argued in the earlier essay, are largely due to the growth of the electronics industry in nearby San Jose, which has an interesting water history of its own. The conversion of the Santa Clara Valley (with San Jose at its center) into the Silicon Valley is an example of how imported water tears a region away from its natural limits, and leads to all manner of bizarre social and ecological formations. It is now a cliché to compare the smog and sprawl of San Jose to similar horrors in Los Angeles. What is not generally recognized is that San Jose is just as dependent on imported water as its southland soulmate. Although 50 percent of Santa Clara Valley's water comes from wells, those wells are recharged by percolation ponds fed by water from the Sierras and delivered

opponents of imported water ever do manage to make it a debate), remember that the local owners of Pajaro Valley land will be reluctant to put any big bucks into a water plan that produces water which can not be consumed by a future suburbia.

The possibility that San Luis water would be imported in the name of agriculture, and then used for development, was first pointed out by Santa Cruz County Supervisor Gary Patton in 1984, when the PVWMA was being established. His objections led to a legislative amendment that ties San Luis water to agricultural uses. But once the water is here, as Patton himself has acknowledged, no words on a piece of paper will effectively limit its use.

I do not mean to say that imported water is inevitable. Far from it. It requires, at the very least, the approval of Pajaro Valley voters, and expenditures of large sums of public money. Even if voters approve and the money is found, there is no guarantee that the water will be delivered. San Luis water is part of the California Water Project, the very same water that agribusiness and environmentalists recently have been squabbling about in Sacramento and Washington D.C. As powerful as our own agri-industry may be, we could easily lose out in future negotiations to even more powerful forces in California's Hydraulic Empire.

---

by state, federal, and Yuba County water projects. The Santa Clara Valley Water District estimates that since the mid-1980s more than 90 percent of the water used in the valley has been imported. One might argue that importing water was the crucial human manipulation of nature necessary to create the Silicon Valley. Without imported water as a substitute, the computer industry would not have been able to destroy Santa Clara Valley's own water supply with chlorinated cleaning solvent poisons.

Officially, nothing is decided. Michael Armstrong, director of PVWMA, stresses that all reasonable options — including suspension of pumping along the coast, a College Lake Dam, injection wells, and reclaimed water — are still being considered. The public, he assures us, will have the final say.

Nevertheless, we have to hope that contradictions within the Empire's ruling groups, or lack of capital, will save us from imported water. I see very little evidence that any local movement can stop it. At the two PVWMA meetings I attended, the public's only appearance was on a magnified flowchart in a series of boxes labeled "public input." One arrow pointed into the boxes, another led out of them. Public input, whatever that may be, is not going to interfere with their plans.

Don't get me wrong. People did attend the meetings. But they did not constitute a "public." They were people with direct economic interest in the project, people whose main sentiment seemed to be best expressed by local grower Ray Travers: "Let's stop this messing around and get that water here as soon as we can."

Decide for yourself. Drive down Highway 1, up over the little ridge that rims the Pajaro Valley's south end, past Dominic's Vegetable Stand, past the home-made castle overlooking Moss Landing, and down to L&S surplus with all the flags flying. That's Struve Road. Take Struve to Giberson, and follow Giberson to Zmudouski State Beach.

Park in the parking lot, and walk 200 yards north on the dirt road along the lagoon, to the first furrowed field. Step off the distance through the dunes to the high tide line. It is less than 75 yards, by my count. Judge the elevation of the farm land. Isn't it below sea level? Walk back through the dunes and pick up a handful of the furrowed earth. What you will have is a handful of sand. These people are farming sand dunes! Irrigated water runs straight through it. Phenomenal amounts of water must be used here.

Now cast your eyes up and to the east. Do you see the hills in the distance? That is the southern end of the Santa Cruz Mountains, about ten miles away from where you are standing. The San Luis Dam is more than 60 miles beyond those hills. And the plan is to bring water down from the reservoir, through those mountains, to water the fields at your feet.

I have one disclaimer. There is no argument here against irrigation. When I discussed these questions with Lauro Navarro, a displaced Green Giant worker who now works in the strawberries, he warned me about just that.

"You know, Frank, many people come here from Mexico because of water. In my home town, San Pedro Tesistan, Jalisco, there is no irrigation. When it rains, people eat, when it doesn't, people go hungry. There's nothing wrong with pumping water from the ground and irrigating crops."

Right. What is wrong is profit-driven overpumping to irrigate water-craving crops grown in dunes of sand. And importing water to turn Pajaro Valley into a suburb of the Valley of Silicon.

(April, 1992)

(Photo: Bill Lovejoy/Santa Cruz Sentinel)

10

Small Time Slumlord Learned
Tricks of Trade on City Payroll

How many of you remember back in mid-July when a fire at Lincoln and High streets destroyed four small apartments housing 37 people? The fire was reported in three consecutive front page articles in the *Register-Pajaronian,* which taken together formed what is fast becoming a cliché: Some disaster ("natural" or otherwise) reveals to the world that poor people in Watsonville live in overcrowded, overpriced, unsafe, illegal housing.

The stories, well put together by reporters Emilio Alvarado and Susanna Heckman, had one new twist. The owner of the building, one Dennis H. Miller, when asked about the fact that the downstairs apartment was zoned commercially, and therefore was illegally rented as housing, responded that the building is managed by the Century 21 real estate agency of Johnson, Roach, and Hansen, and that they were the responsible parties. Joel Roach, of Century 21, countered that his agency only collects the rent and that Miller is the one to be held accountable. How amusing to see a couple of real-life partners in crime falling all over themselves to turn one another in.

We never learned the ultimate outcome of this grotesque charade. "City and fire officials are continuing their investigation," we were told in the concluding article, and that is the last word on the subject that ever appeared in print.

But it is not quite the end of the story. My friend Mike Kostyal and I looked into it a little bit further, and here's what we found.

Dennis H. Miller, the owner of the building, used to be a building inspector for the city of Watsonville. He was first hired in 1966 as an engineering aide, and worked his way up to Inspector in 1978. For the next ten and a half years one of his main responsibilities was to enforce the Watsonville building code. In this same period he bought five houses himself. He rents four, of which three are multi-unit properties.

In January 1989, one of those properties was discovered to be in clear violation of the building code: It contained dangerous wiring, sleeping quarters too close to gas burning appliances, an illegally overcrowded room, three electrical meters and one gas meter illegally installed, and a single family unit illegally converted to a duplex.

All of this on a property owned by Mr. Miller at the same time that his job was to enforce the building code.

What happened? Nothing much. In a deal arranged by that great guardian of the public trust, ex-city manager John Radin, Mr. Miller was allowed to resign in good standing with full pension rights, and was guaranteed a positive job recommendation. City officials also promised they would make no public disclosure of any of the particulars of his case. His only penalty was that he could never again work for the city of Watsonville.

The result of such light "punishment?" Mr. Miller went right on maintaining illegal and unsafe rentals. To this day the property that was originally cited back in January 1989 has not been brought fully up to code, and the rent from one of the units there is now paid to the city of Watsonville, rather than to Miller. In this way the city hopes to pressure Miller to obey the law. Although whenever he does fully comply with the law, all the rent (minus 10 percent) will be returned to him, as specified by city ordinance.

In the midst of this little tug of war, the fire broke out at Lincoln and High, revealing the other illegal rental owned by Miller. Exactly what was the violation there? People were living in a commercially zoned space which, among other things, had neither enough windows nor adequate ventilation. The significance of this was not lost on Fire Captain Jim Norwood, who told the *Register-Pajaronian* that the fire was potentially dangerous because of the amount of smoke and that "fortunately the fire happened at a time no one was sleeping and residents noticed the smoke immediately and got out safely."

What we have here is a near tragedy, in an unsafe and illegal rental owned by an ex-building inspector who lost his job with the city for maintaining just such units. And what does the city propose to do now? Nothing, according to City Attorney Luis Hernandez. As long as the commercial space is not illegally rented again, the city plans no further (!) action against Mr. Miller.

While tracking this story, I talked to many people about Dennis Miller. No one was willing to defend him publicly. A few offered pale excuses for what he had done. Miller, they said, is by no means the worst landlord in town. He probably got messed up in this because as a building inspector he saw what was really happening in the local housing market. As one of his tepid defenders put it: "Dennis figured if everyone else was doing it, why not him."

Yes, it is true that the crime is built into the system, and that Dennis Miller is not one of the big boys who makes the system work. Rather he was just a corrupt, small town building inspector who took advantage of his position to make some bucks for himself.

Nor did Dennis Miller do much to defend himself the one time I talked to him in person. I found him on a construction job in town, working on an addition to a house. A robust, middle-aged man, with carpenter's bags on his hips, he was leading a crew of younger workers.

I asked him about the Lincoln Street fire.

"There have been a lot of untrue facts in the paper about that fire."

"Like what?"

"No comment."

I asked him about the unit zoned commercial that was being used for housing.

"I can't be responsible for what people do in my houses. I rented that out as storage."

"At $350 a month?"

"No comment."

I asked him about his early retirement from the building department, and that agitated him.

"I have no comment on that, and I don't want any of this in the newspapers. I have to live in this town and get along with everybody and I don't want this in the papers."

After that it was "no comment" to every question, and I finally left.

I have no specific suggestion for what would be Mr. Miller's just deserts. Nor do I take any great pleasure in telling this story. Dennis Miller is small potatoes, his crimes and misdemeanors second page material. And yet our town suffers from his petty triumphs, as he lives in his own lovely $250,000 home off the money he makes on run-down rentals.

Perhaps those who will be most offended by the Dennis Miller story are the honest landlords and landladies who also benefit from the free market in housing, but at least try to live within its rules. Like the woman I was standing next to at City Hall when I first learned that Dennis Miller had been a building inspector. This elderly lady, with thick glasses and a heavy Slavonian accent, dutifully had come to the Building Department to check if she could convert a room over her garage into a legal rental.

When the information about Miller came out, I was so surprised that I was physically knocked off balance, and I plopped into a chair next to the counter. The would-be landlady, who had overheard the crucial information about Miller, came over to me, bent down, and touched my arm as if to comfort me. Her milky blue pupils, greatly magnified by thick glasses, were just inches from my face. In an unsteady, but loud and angry voice, she spat out her judgement of this case:

"Shame on that man. Shame on him."

(December, 1990)

Old time mansion *(Photo: Jon Silver)*

11

Progress and Poverty
Come to Watsonville

A re there still some "single-taxers" out there? I have been thinking about Henry George quite a bit these days, as Watsonville bangs its head up against the contradiction of the need for low-income housing versus the high price of land. George, born in 1839 before the United States became an industrial country, was a junior high school drop-out from a poor family. A transplanted Californian, he made his living as a San Francisco printer and journalist. He became one of the world's leading social reformers, and although his movement all but disappeared in the early part of this century, it is still possible (and usually a pleasure) to find among us some crazed enthusiast of his great gimmick: the single tax on land.

George's argument went something like this. Private monopoly of land is both an ethical outrage and an economic disaster. It is morally repugnant because "...the equal right of all men to the use of land is as clear as their equal right to breathe the air....it is a right which is natural and inalienable...and can be limited only by the equal rights of others."

Or, as God put it, back in the days when God was around and Henry could score a point or two by quoting him:

"And they should build houses and inhabit them; and they shall plant vineyards and eat the fruits of them. They shall not build and another inhabit; they shall not plant and another eat." (Isaiah 65: 21-22)

Not only is private ownership of land an affront to these quaint old ideas of God, natural rights, and public morality, but, according to George, it is also responsible for poverty.

Henry's theory of poverty was rooted in the American frontier. George was here in California when this outrageously plentiful land which had been taken from the Indians, and then from the Mexicans, was being given by the American government to the "Railroad Barons" and "Cattle Kings." Henry argued that as long as only a few were here to use it, the land was relatively cheap. As the land filled up, as people began to work it, as civilization developed, the land became valuable. Not through the effort of the dear landlord, but rather through the collective effort of the whole community.

The "Land Lords," however, hold title to the land and charge the rest of us increasingly high "rents" (or set high sales prices) which swallow up nearly all that we make through our own efforts. Thus, just like vassals (interesting how these feudal terms—Barons, Kings, Lords—cropped up in the ordinary language of a supposedly democratic country), we work to make the Land Lords rich, and as civilization advances, poverty increases.

Progress and Poverty, George called his great work, and although no publishing house would take it and he had to print the first edition himself, eventually more copies of the book were sold than of any other work on economics in the English language.

And out of that book, his followers constructed a great plan: through a single tax on land we could take the unjust "rent" from the Land Lords, and use it for the general good of the community. All other taxes and means of raising revenue would be unnecessary. Through this one large tax, old Hank would effectively expropriate the Land Lords without the social upheaval that would come from actually seizing their land.

It was a big idea which promised revolutionary change through a single reform. The single tax movement spread from the West Coast to the East Coast, from New York to Ireland and back again. The movement made Henry George a distinguished man of letters and almost made him mayor of New York.

Eventually the single-taxers were defeated. George had missed the point that exploitation can also be based on the ownership of factories, and his movement became isolated from the urban working class. His theory remains today a fading memory, kept alive by a few fanatics operating out of a handful of Henry George Schools.

So why am I disturbing old Hank's bones? Why this little discourse in American historical biography?

At the risk of seeming an old crank, I invite you to look at Watsonville from what is left of Henry's eyes.

(1) In the mere twenty years that I have lived around here, I have seen progress and poverty grow apace. Watsonville and the Pajaro Valley are both richer and poorer than they were in 1970. A higher percentage of people live in what once were called mansions, and a growing number live in garages and made-over chicken coops. Every year the agricultural commissioner reports higher gross receipts for the Pajaro Valley (over $300 million in 1989), while the number of poor farmworkers increases. In one possible (probable?) future, Watsonville will have moved, in a single generation, from a moderately prosperous working class town to an increasingly popular California combination on the menu: a wealthy bedroom community sitting next to a Mexican slum. If you want to envision what we might look like after 20 more years of

piecemeal replacement of agricultural land by $300,000 townhouses, think of Palo Alto and East Palo Alto. What could be more Georgian?

(2) Isn't Proposition 13 an almost direct inverse of the single tax on land? By that infamous 1978 law we can't increase the tax on land to reflect its true market value, so as a community we can't benefit from our overall economic development. Land taxation is limited, so we have to cut back on libraries, schools, community centers, parks, you name it. Sounds suspiciously like mandated progress and poverty to me.

(3) The price of an acre of downtown land is reported to be $600,000. Once you spend that much money, how can you make good on your investment? Build for rich people. Henry George would appreciate the irony: The high price of land makes any sensible use of it impossible.

The list could go on. Once you start looking through Henry's particular prism, it is surprising what you can see. I leave you with one last argument.

Back in the 1870s, Henry George argued that as a legal entity, San Francisco owned all the land within its city limits. Individual people might hold land titles, but their "private rights to land should always be held subordinate to the general good." Under extreme conditions this principle is embodied in the government's right of eminent domain; George argued that in ordinary times the community's claim to the land should be used to generate public revenues.

Watsonville faces what seems an insurmountable contradiction. Land is so expensive to acquire that low-cost housing is impossible to build. We might be able to put a few units here or there, but not nearly the number necessary for the "general good."

How to find land for low-cost housing?

We need not bring out the stick of eminent domain. Our city already has title to 290 acres of undeveloped, non-agricultural land, beautifully located for housing. We do not have to take it away from anyone. This land (enough room for thousands of housing units, a few parks, and a couple of schools) already belongs to us as a community. I speak, of course, of the Watsonville Municipal Airport.

According to the *Register-Pajaronian*, the mere suggestion of using airport land for housing brought gasps from 90 people at a Board of Realtors luncheon. That is to be expected. Real estate speculators and Land Lords have no interest in the construction of low-income houses. A larger supply of inexpensive homes would make it harder for them to sell homes at exorbitant rates. It wouldn't take the food off their tables, but it might take the extra BMW out of their garages.

Nevertheless, it is perfectly reasonable to urge the real estate people to join the debate on low-income housing, as our new Mayor did at the very same luncheon, as long as we keep in mind that asking them to debate low-income housing is like asking the hounds to debate how fast the fox should be allowed to run.

But a debate is what it should be. Let's decide the future of the airport through political discourse and mobilization, rather than through some reference to bureaucratic regulation, as some in city government are now doing. A perfect example is the claim that we can't close down the airport because we would have to repay the federal government for all the airport improvements they have laid out over the years. That is not the way to open a discussion, that is the way to close one.

Here is an *opening* question: What other plan is there for preserving prime agricultural land and building a sufficient number of low-income houses?

(March, 1990)

200 block of Main Street before demolition
(Photo: Kurt Ellison/Register-Pajaronian)

$$\overline{12}$$

The Post Office Wins a Prize

The Watsonville Beautification Committee, whatever that may be, has declared our new post office, "Commercial Building of the Month," which leaves me wondering what was runner-up — Long's parking lot?

"Modern Prison Institutional" is the way I would describe the new building. Made of nondescript brick and concrete block, it sits behind a drive-through lane and a small parking lot, and was designed, with the help of a computer no doubt, to fit seamlessly anywhere in these fifty united states.

Inside is even worse, with not one decorative tile nor brick. A mural of local history, like the ones that grace so many 1930s WPA post offices, was too much to ask, but couldn't we have had some indication that someone involved in this project had taken into account Watsonville's climate or culture or history?

And the lines are as long as ever. Although the Feds were willing to spend big bucks buying land and throwing together a building, they are unwilling to spend any extra dollars to hire new clerks. So around noon—given post office hours and the hours most of us work, the only time we can get inside the damn place — you still wait as long as half an hour to get to a window.

Not that you could check such a thing by looking at the clock on the wall. Like any police interrogation room, there is no clock. Are they too cheap? Are they protecting themselves from possible riots from Watsonvillians counting up wasted hours waiting in line? Do they not want their workers to "watch the clock"? Or is it all part of a grand design to place the building, like the perfect prison, outside ordinary coordinates of space and time?

The post office now squats, next to a fenced-in empty lot, on what was once the 200 block of Main Street. A working class, Mexican and Filipino mini-community, it included Anthony's Fish Market (by far the best in town, with nothing yet to replace it), St. Vincent De Paul, two Mexican bars, the Filipene Gardens, a barber shop, an appliance store, a surplus store, a couple of small retail outlets specializing in clothes and tools, Discoteca (the best Mexican book and record store in town), three cheap restaurants including the old Jalisco (better food at almost half the price than you now pay three blocks "uptown" at the new Jalisco), two tire outlets and one garage, some run-down low-income housing, and a lively street life.

Not the earthquake, but the wrecker's ball and taxpayers' money tumbled down this little neighborhood. Ex-City Manager John Radin engineered this disastrous redevelopment deal in which the city paid more than $6,500,000 to buy and destroy the block, and then sold half of it to the Post Office for $1,750,000 and the other half to San Jose developer Barry Swenson for $250,000 down and a note for $650,000.

Yes, the numbers are right. Even if Swenson pays off the note (two and a half years after he signed it, he still hasn't begun to do so) the city will have lost $4 million on the deal. Not to mention the jobs that are gone, the low-income housing destroyed rather than refurbished, and the sales tax revenue lost.

Why did the city throw away so much money? For Radin and the old city council (led by local realtor and ex-city councilman Rex Clark), the Mexican/Filipino neighborhood sitting right across from City Hall was an embarrassment; destroying it was a good place to begin the planned gentrification of Watsonville.

Too bad for them, and lucky for us, there are not enough gentry around. On the northwest side of town, many new expensive homes sit unsold. And—surprise of all surprises—Barry Swenson is unable to find any classy retail stores that want to locate in downtown Watsonville. Meanwhile the new city council—prodded by the current representative of the real estate industry in City Hall, Tony Campos, who knows a bad deal when he sees one—met in mid-December in closed session to try to figure out what to do about the whole bloody mess.

There's nothing to do. The old 200 block, and the four million dollars that were spent to destroy it, are gone forever. Now the planners have other deals to put together. A new scheme involves the old post office—a charming, two story building that fit perfectly with the downtown plaza. The city recently bought this deserted beauty for $425,000.

And what do they want to do with it? Their current plan is to use it for another fancy Mexican restaurant —"to bring people downtown," they say. The right kind of people of course. Those who will pay too much money to eat bland food, seasoned with enough salsa to market the planners' new dream for downtown: a quaint little Old Town, where tourists will come to buy prettied up pieces of slaughtered Mexican culture.

(January, 1992)

Politics

(Photo: Diane Varni/Register-Pajaronian)

$\overline{13}$

Earthquake Politics:
From Mexico City to Watsón

I was standing outside and saw a chimney collapse at the house I had just left, but my most lasting memory of the first day was Candy Dunne walking down our street, long hair loose behind her, wrench in hand, calmly helping people turn off their gas lines. No panic gripped the 20-some people standing in the street, and some of us had already turned off our gas, but Candy's competence put many of us at ease, even as the black smoke from a destroyed mobile home darkened the sky over our heads.

We lost five homes on the 200 block of Prospect Street. They jumped off their foundations and split their floors. Living in those five homes were nine Mexican families: two of the houses were owned by the people who lived in them, the other three were rentals. Of the nine families, one returned to Mexico, two moved to another rental in Salinas, four now live with relatives in other parts of Watsonville, and two are camping behind their wrecked home in the backyard next to ours.

While the earthquake physically wrecked our block and dislodged about one-tenth of our numbers, it also made us into a neighborhood. People who usually do little more than nod to each other, immediately began to share food, water, and medicine. Later we moved easily in and out of one another's homes, helping as much as we could. Most everyone spent the first night in the local park, huddled around big fires, sharing food and blankets, minding the neighborhood kids, and swapping stories. Between us, we speak four languages in the immediate area around Floodberg Park—Spanish, English, Serbo-Croatian, and Portuguese—but most people come from Mexico or further south. One of the main topics of conversation was "other quakes I have lived through" with a few people telling of greater shocks in Mexico City in '85 or El Salvador in '76.

The next day was spent cleaning up. About mid-day two men arrived in a flat-bed truck carrying two large tents, one that fit 30 people and one that could house 100. They gave us the one for 30, and we spent a couple of hours together setting it up. It now sits in my neighbors' backyard, providing shelter for four children under five, two women (one pregnant) and three men.

"Who are you guys?" I asked the men who had brought the tent, as we were putting it up.

"Mike and Jim, " said the larger man, the only one of the two who put more than one sentence together at a time.

"Just Mike and Jim?"

"Yep, just Mike and Jim from Benecia."

"When do you want the tent back?"

"Whenever you are done with it. One week, two weeks, two years, whenever."

They offered us the tent for 100 people, but our street didn't need it. I suggested that they call Migrant Media to see where to put it up.

"No," said Mike, "we don't deal with no agencies. This is people to people."

People to people is what it was all week. One of the neighborhood landladies brought sacks of groceries to her tenants, several times cars simply drove through the neighborhood dropping off food, blankets, and clean drinking water. I asked one of the people who was unloading green plastic bags filled with much desired Pampers where she was from.

She put her forefinger to her lips.

"Shhh. We are not supposed to be doing this. But I'll be damned if I will sit there with a warehouse full of stuff, when there are people out here who need it."

Those first night stories of the 1985 Mexico City quake stayed with me all week. In my neighborhood, we were living, in miniature, what had happened in Mexico. The Mexican Quake was 8.1 on the Richter scale, more than ten times greater than what we felt in Watsonville. From 5,000 to 50,000 people died (depending on whom you believe) and miles of the city tumbled down. But in the midst of the rubble, Mexicans found a new political understanding of themselves. Throughout the city — not just for a couple of nights, but for weeks — people within their neighborhoods and on their own initiative took care of each other. They organized rescue teams who worked with pick and shovel to save people buried beneath downed buildings. They distributed medicine and food; people organized waste disposal and sanitation crews. They set up neighborhood shelters, they cared for the injured, and gave solace to those who lost families.

While the people were taking care of business, the government either did nothing or actually interfered with the rescue efforts. In the first 12 hours there was no official comment or action whatsoever. President Miguel de la Madrid, holed up in his residence at Los Pinos, did not address the country until 36 hours after the first shock. When the police and army finally hit the streets, they cordoned off areas and tried to prevent rescue teams from entering damaged buildings. Neither the army nor the police ever worked with pick and shovel; rather they protected the bulldozers that were brought in to finish off the destruction. When some elements of the police started to sell rescue supplies arriving in Mexico from around the world, neighborhood committees went straight to the airport and confiscated the cargos as they came off the planes, and then distributed them through their own newly-emerged organizations.

The experience was so intense that it changed the Mexican language. The two words *"sociedad civil"* which before the earthquake had been used only in rather obscure political discourse, became common currency. They came to mean, in the words of Carlos Monsiváis, *"el esfuerzo comunitario de autogestión y solidaridad, el espacio independiente del gobierno..."* ("self-generated community power and solidarity, the space independent of the government").

And just as that phrase was used over and over by political commentators to explain what was happening, in the streets the meaning of the word *"chilango"* changed forever. A *chilango* is a native of Mexico City, and until September 19, 1985, the day of the earthquake, it was a term of derision. A week later people were saying with pride, *"soy chilango."* Pride in the fact that despite the horror of the disaster, despite the active opposition of the government, the people of Mexico City had organized their own rescue and recovery. I felt a little of that same pride when I saw Candy walking down the street, accompanied by a few people of the neighborhood, shutting off the gas. Hey, we can do it here on Prospect Street, here in Watsonville, we need neither experts nor government officials, we can take care of ourselves.

In Mexico, the high of solidarity and cooperation lasted for several weeks. Those weeks fundamentally changed Mexican politics. The political self-confidence that Mexicans found amidst the disaster, coupled with the government's corruption and helplessness, made the Cárdenas campaign and the PRD's electoral challenge to PRI possible.

In Watsonville, the exhilaration that comes from human solidarity lasted only a few days. What its long-term political effects will be, nobody knows.

It is no exaggeration to say that before the quake Watsonville stood at a crucial moment in its history. On the one side we have the political consciousness developed in last year's frozen-food workers' strike, plus the imminent replacement of the Anglo, business-oriented city council by a district elected council on which Mexican and working class neighborhoods will have some official voice. On the other side, in opposition to these forces, are large real estate interests that want to transform Watsonville into a rich bedroom community for San Jose, displacing Mexican workers and destroying our agricultural lands.

In the midst of that struggle, the quake hit, damaging much of downtown, whose future was already being contested by community and real estate groups; it also destroyed more than 400 houses, the majority of which were in poorer neighborhoods and housed the very people the realtors want to remove.

Watsonville will be rebuilt. But in what way, and guided by which principles? I suggest we look to the example of Mexico, and I close this little essay with four demands, essentially burrowed from the neighborhood councils that sprang up in the damaged *vecindades* and *barrios* of Mexico City.

(1) Full distribution of all relief supplies. No warehouses full of tents while people sleep in cars.

(2) Massive construction of low-income housing, with the building being done, as much as possible, by the people who will live in those houses.

(3) Everyone (renter, leasee, owner) has the right to return to the place they were living or doing business before the quake, in whatever structure is rebuilt on that spot.

(4) No structure that can be rebuilt should be destroyed. We do not want a brand new town. We want to save as much as we can of our old one.

(November, 1989)

Children at school district demonstration
(Photo: Kurt Ellison/Register-Pajaronian)

14

Where Does the Money Go?

For the past several weeks a couple of hundred teachers, other school employees, and parents have fought a good little battle inside the Pajaro Valley Unified School District. Some two hundred of us overwhelmed a couple of board meetings — banging sticks, chanting slogans, applauding our friends, even hissing our enemies. In a forum usually reserved for tedious, jargon-ridden nit-picking, we made clear and passionate arguments, articulate pleas, and specific proposals in real language. Or so it seemed to me.

Petitions, small meetings, leaflets, big meetings, juicy gossip, fast-travelling rumors and jokes, serious conversations among people who rarely get the chance to talk to each other, we had it all: a taste of genuinely democratic politics.

We won more than we lost. We forced the school board to give the teachers a five percent raise, instead of the three percent they intended to give. (The extra two percent automatically extends to classified workers, too.) We pressured the union officials to push harder for the stipend for extra credentials (the stipend issue is mostly about the district's slow betrayal of bilingual teaching and teachers). And finally we raised so many questions about the school district budget that the board was obliged to schedule a November 20th meeting with only one item on the agenda: how to cut administrative expenses. None of this would have happened without our mini-movement.

Within each victory there was also a defeat. Our "raise" is no raise at all, as it does not even keep up with inflation. Although the AFT is now taking a stronger line on the stipend, once again, we didn't get it. And although we have a meeting on administrative cuts coming up, the school board immediately used our wage hike as an excuse to make two million dollars in unnecessary cuts of basic programs and services in the schools.

The key word is "unnecessary." While it is true that the state legislature is slowly strangling public education, it is also true that plenty of money is wasted in local school districts. The PVUSD is no exception.

Our school district receives almost $70 million from the State of California and other sources. At last report, 16,275 students were enrolled. That means the district gets more than $4,000 to educate each student. With about 30 students in a class (there are actually a few more) that makes approximately $120,000 of resources per classroom.

What a joke. Only about half of that $120,000 is taken up by the salaries and benefits of the teachers, aides, custodians, and secretaries whose work is essential to each classroom. Another small percentage goes for the materials available to those workers. The rest is eaten up in the administrative fiddle-faddle of a bloated educational bureaucracy.

Look at the district office on Blackburn Street. A lot of necessary work gets done there — mostly by low paid secretaries and clerks. But those offices also house nineteen (19!) Superintendents, Assistant Superintendents, Special Assistants to the Superintendents, Directors, and Assistant Directors, none of whom have any regular contact with students.

Many (not all) of these self-described "educators" keep themselves busy in meeting after meeting, luncheon after luncheon, talking over the popular slogans of the day: "restructuring" and "strategic planning" are currently in fashion, before that it was "self-esteem," and when I came back into teaching nine years ago, it was "back to basics." These conversations are almost endless, filled with incomprehensible educationese, suck up hundreds of thousands of dollars (if not more), and accomplish almost nothing. Their main purpose is to justify the ever expanding number of top administrators, and to make them feel they deserve their big salaries and large expense accounts.

It is not easy to find this wasted money in the school district budget. Part of the purpose of the budget of a public agency is to hide where the money goes, and there are no line items labelled "Administrative Fiddle-Faddle" or "Meaningless Meetings."

Nevertheless, we have learned a lot in the last several weeks of struggle, and we have found a few embarrassing figures. School board member Kristen Cozad has focused on the mini-imperial style of Superintendent Merill Grant, whose office is budgeted for $358,000.

Cozad has come up with some telling comparisons. Grant's personal mileage allowance is $7,500 (30,000 miles a year at 25 cents a mile) while the mileage allowance for school field trips varies from a high of $1,755 at Aptos High School to a low of $151 at Alianza. His "other supplies" and "other expenses" add up to $22,000, exactly the amount that was saved earlier this year by eliminating the insurance that covered students who are accidently injured at school.

But it is too easy to cap on Merrill, an obvious public relations fraud and two-bit bully. The problem is systemic; Merrill is only part of it.

During the last set of negotiations, the AFT found other budget figures fully as damaging as Grant's padded official expenses. How does a $1,800,000 slush fund grab you?

It is a little complicated, but worth going through the numbers. In the 1990-'91 Budget, the district planned to spend 2,395,263 "unrestricted" dollars on line item #4300, "Instructional Materials and Supplies." In fact, that year they spent only 595,358 "unrestricted" dollars on that item. That makes $1,800,905 that was transferred out of that account to some place else. Did they make an adjustment in '91-'92, scaling down their budget to reflect what they had spent the year before? No. Rather, for this year they have budgeted 2,4054,137 "unrestricted" dollars for the same thing.

Get the drift? They knowingly overbudget an important sounding item and then use the extra money any way they please. A classic slush fund, it is no doubt the source of some of the "discretionary funds" that the top administrators use to increase their power and prestige.

Of course, in a budget of $70 million, not every penny can be spent as planned. Money has to move from account to account; it would be impossible to operate if it couldn't. Nor is there any evidence than anybody is doing anything illegal. As far as we know, nobody has vacationed in Tahiti on our children's money.

Nevertheless, the administration should be able to tell us where the $1,800,000 went last year, especially when they have overbudgeted by almost the same amount this year. But according to the union negotiators, when they asked for an accounting of this money, the administration declined.

Meanwhile, the schools are suffering a shortage of exactly what line item #4300 is supposed to buy. At Freedom School, for example, each teacher has $500 per year to pay for basic supplies. These include pencils, paper, chalk, staples, and two cents a copy for use of the school copy machine. Peggy Morrison, who teaches second grade at Freedom, reports that she has to spend a minimum of $30 a month of her own money just keep her classroom going.

Peggy Morrison's story is not unusual. Ask any teacher. Or better yet, join together with the teachers, parents, and classified employees of the district on Wednesday, November 20th at Aptos High School at 7:30 PM, when administrative cuts will be officially on the agenda.

Together we may be able to squeeze some money out of the "educators" in order to help educate our kids.

(November, 1991)

(Photo: Kurt Ellison/Register-Pajaronian)

15

Democracy and its Enemies

We do not live in a democracy; in Watsonville, and in the United States of America, the people (*demos*) do not rule (*kratos*). This is not exactly news. But during our recent struggles with local educational bureaucrats, we got some new evidence about just how anti-democratic our society has become.

The people are assumed to be stupid. Most of the school board, and all the top bureaucrats, think that ordinary people can not understand the school budget. Sherree Brown, Supervisor of Accounting, introduced her special presentation of the budget by calling it "complicated and technical." Bob Peterson, Assistant Superintendent in charge of Business Services, described a J-200 form as "complicated...difficult to understand." For these administrators, "explaining" the budget to parents was a waste of time, like trying to teach astrophysics to preschoolers.

The budget, however, is put together in such a way as to make it hard to understand. Most of the recent confusion came from the fact that the official school district budget does not list actual expenditures. That last fact is worth restating. The budget of the Pajaro Valley Unified School District, the one made available to parents and used by the school board to oversee district spending, lists last year's Adopted Budget and next year's Proposed Budget, but does not show last year's Actual Expenditures. The district also keeps no public record of budget transfers, making it impossible to track money as it moves from padded accounts (like Instructional Materials and Supplies) to become discretionary money in the misleadingly low accounts of the top administrators.

Thus, it took our parent group many hours adding up scores of columns in computer print-outs to determine that last year the superintendent's office actually spent $461,387.03, although the Adopted Budget lists him as spending $290, 337.00. Furthermore, given the current budget process, we have no way of knowing from which accounts those extra dollars came.

The budget process, as it now exists, is thoroughly and completely anti-democratic. Much like modern cars which are built so that they cannot be worked on by ordinary backyard mechanics, the PVUSD budget is computed in such a way that is hard to follow all the hoses, belts, and wires. Having constructed it that way, the money people in the district then tell us we should not waste our (and their) time trying to understand the budget, but rather leave it to the experts who alone can comprehend its mysterious secrets.

One of the basic faiths of democracy is that regular people can understand public issues. It is a common criticism of our age that public decisions have become so complicated that we must rely on the opinions of experts and technicians. What the struggle over the school budget revealed is that the experts and technicians inside the PVUSD make no attempt to present the money figures in a simple, easy to understand format, and thereby ensure their continued liberty to make decisions free of school board and public control.

Some people have the right to vote and some people don't. School district election laws not only guarantee over-representation of the affluent and under-representation of the poor, but also entirely disqualify large numbers of potential voters. This is the way it works. Of the 60 to 75 percent of the parents in the district who are Latino, perhaps as many as half of them are not legal citizens of the United States. They are full members of the community, taxpayers and workers who produce much of the Pajaro Valley's wealth, people who have lived in the area for many years, but not citizens and not eligible to vote in any election. This is the fundamental fact about all Watsonville politics (not just school district politics) and it is one of the main ways the old ruling groups stay in control.

On top of this, the school district refuses to institute genuine district elections, which would improve the chances of some Latino representation on the board. (The school board currently does not have any Latino member, although the students are overwhelmingly Mexican and Latino.) District elections, just like the district election in the city of Watsonville, would not solve the problem of disenfranchised non-citizen members of the community, but it would be a small step toward democracy.

The incredible rudeness of the school board toward parents—the most recent example was making 300 people wait for hours, until literally the middle of the night, for their item to come up on the agenda—can only be understood when you take into account that the school board members know that the vast majority of those 300 people have no right to vote them out of office.

Grim? Certainly. Hopeless? No. People rule (democracy) has rarely appeared in the world as anything more than an ideal, as the hope of the oppressed, as the essential goal of *los de abajo.* No democratic institutions have lasted very long in the world, and even the best institutions never guarantee true people power. Democracy always depends on the continuing participation of the people, themselves, people hungry for collective self-rule.

And by those standards, we scored a few democratic victories here in little old Watsonville in the last few months. When Ingrid Obrecht, a parent concerned about the education of her children, found the $326,000 "computer error" in the budget (a mistake that had gone unrecognized by all the experts and technicians in our school district), that was a victory for democracy. When more than 300 parents showed up at the school board meeting, demanding that the found $326,000 be used to restore bus service for their kids, that was a victory for democracy. And finally, when the parents' group decided not to wait for School Board approval of our demand No.11 ("a community oversight committee will be formed and will become an integral part of the budget process") but rather, simply declared ourselves the new Budget Oversight Committee, and then proved it by doing it, that was a victory for democracy.

So it gives me great pleasure as an official member (membership is open to all who attend meetings) of the PVUSD Budget Oversight Committee to invite all members of the community to the next school board meeting on Wednesday, December 11, at 7:30 PM, at Aptos High School, where we will continue our fight for democratic schools in a democratic society.

(December, 1991)

Girl on school bus *(Photo: Kurt Ellison/Register-Pajaronian)*

16

Hey Jaime, Don't Blame the Kids

The stakes are high in *Stand and Deliver*. In the opening frames the hero drives through Los Angeles, leaving a high paying job and a prosperous life for harder work and lower wages teaching at a barrio high school. Through his VW window he sees the life awaiting the failures among his would-be students: selling oranges in the street, riding to a day labor job in the back of a pick-up truck, or just hanging out down these mean streets. A threat lurks behind every scene in his classroom. Drop out of this class and become a chicken man, working with the Colonel.

School: the main place in our two-tier California where if you were not clever enough to be born at the top, you just might be able to work your way to it. School: where we select the few who will have good jobs, decent homes, and enough money not to have to count their pennies in their old age, and where we teach these lucky ones that they *deserve* such lives. School: where we tell the vast majority who will live out their lives in the lower tier that they *deserve* to be there, as they ruined their chances with lack of discipline, or drugs, or early pregnancy, or not working hard enough, or by being just too dumb. School: better odds than the lottery, but not by much.

The hidden trap of *Stand and Deliver* is that our schools exist in a society without enough of the good life to go around. Everyone can't win in school; if everyone won, who would do the dirty work? Who would produce the food, fabricate the aluminum window frames, care for the children, and nurse the old? Those are jobs for the people who lose.

School is all about winners and losers, and learning which one you are.

So it is no surprise that during the presidential debates, George Bush named Jaime Escalante as his No. 1 hero. Why? Not just because Escalante was chairman of Hispanics for Bush, although that was a piece of it. Rather, because he keeps alive the idea that anybody can make it. "You got what it takes, *ese*, I will make you a winner," he says. "You can beat racism and poverty, you can work your way to the top."

George Bush, and his prep school buddies, need this message. They need to keep everyone in the second tier thinking that their children can work their way into the first one; and they especially need that idea's crucial corollary: if you don't make it, you have only yourself to blame.

Ever wonder why we have so many kids in our classes? Ever think, this is crazy, I can't teach all these kids? We are not meant to. We are supposed to find a few special ones and send them on their way to being the first Hispanic this or that. And the rest? The ones we don't have the time or resources to get to? Well, we can't all go to Stanford. Somebody has to cook the fast food on Freedom Boulevard.

The "solution" to the crisis in our schools is not Hero Teachers. If we want good schools, we will have to build a society with enough good jobs, houses, and a secure old age for everyone. That will take a fight, inside and outside our classrooms. My hope for our students is that we can help them see themselves as powerful and effective human beings who will join us in that fight.

(October, 1988)

Mayor Oscar Rios at the Watsonville Airport
(Photo: Mike McCollum/Register-Pajaronian)

17

It's a Class Thing

C inco de Mayo, 1991, the Plaza. It was a good party, there is no denying that. A warm day, plenty of people, good music, delicious food, spirited dancing in the streets. Quite a difference from last year's Chamber of Commerce sponsored "celebration" where a $5 admission fee kept many Mexican families standing behind barricades, watching other people eat and play.

Even the old National Ice and Cold Storage building cooperated. Once a part of Watsonville's booming frozen food industry, it has stood vacant for years, an obvious symbol of that industry's decline. A few days before the party, someone torched it, and on the 3rd and 4th of May a foul smelling black cloud darkened the city, as the fire department decided to let the old relic burn. Miraculously on the 5th of May, the cloud (which later was revealed to be laden with asbestos) disappeared, and we celebrated under clear skies. On the 6th of May, a small cloud and the acrid smell returned.

Forget, for a moment, the cloud's dark presence. Wasn't this celebration a fitting expression of what is being called hereabouts the "Latinization of Watsonville"? You have heard the litany of progress: the new census which officially recognized that Watsonville is more than 60 percent Latino; the judicial redistricting victory which brought a progressive Latino to the city council for the first time ever, and which promises to deliver at least two Latinos to office in the next elections; the growing influence of LULAC (the League of United Latin American Citizens) in city government; Spanish translations at city council meetings, as well as free Spanish classes for city employees; and even the emergence of *El Andar,* itself, an established bilingual monthly, promoting Latino culture and the left/liberal cause.

It all fits together quite nicely. With city council member Oscar Rios and LULAC heavy-hitter Celia Organista as "Grand Marshalls," Cinco De Mayo 1991 seemed only an appetizer for that great rally yet to come when Latinized Watsonville fully emerges as Oscar becomes our first Latino mayor.

Re-enter the cloud. What this triumphant analysis obscures is that for Watsonville's Mexican working class, the last four years (since the 1987 frozen food strike) have been an unmitigated disaster. In the fields, the UFW is but a shadow of its old self (or, in the words of the Ohlone Indians, has lost its shadow entirely). Transformed from a mass movement to a public relations operation, Chavez's farmworkers union now has only one row crop contract, at Sakata Farms. Elsewhere, union contracts have been replaced by labor contractors, and wages have fallen from a high of $7.50 an hour all the way down to $5.

Life in the canneries is even worse, with the industry in a downward spiral of unknown depth. We have lost a thousand jobs since the strike (and as many as 3,000 in the last ten years) and wages are now $6.67 an hour, down about a half dollar from when the strike began.

The loss of cannery jobs, combined with an increased number of immigrants fleeing Mexico's grim economic crisis, means than even Watsonville's one sure protection against abject poverty — strawberry picking — is no longer enough, as the fields are overrun with too many people chasing too few jobs.

Nor does it stop with fewer jobs at lower wages. Rents rise, welfare benefits are cut, social service agencies are in perpetual crisis, and the schools continue to produce more dropouts than graduates.

It's a class thing. As a small number of Latino businessmen and professionals have gained ground in city politics, Mexican workers and their families — who make up perhaps 40 percent of the town's population and whose labor is responsible for its wealth — fall further behind.

It would be wrong, however, to hold the new Latino/Liberal alliance responsible for economic disaster in the Mexican community. Although it is true that this informal concert has majority control of the city council, the council's power is limited. The real rulers in town (and the people truly responsible for our economic troubles) are the transnationals who dominate local agribusiness, the old timers (mostly Yugoslavians) who still own much of the land of the Pajaro Valley, and the large real estate developers who are trying to turn Watsonville into an upscale bedroom community for San Jose.

But the council is not totally a ceremonial, symbolic body. It does have some independent power, some room to maneuver, some ability to shape Watsonville's future. How will this limited power be used? Who will it help?

This question is yet to be decided, but the early indications are not good. A basic problem here is that politicians, of almost any stripe, want to be elected, and then re-elected. At the same time, Watsonville's working class does not vote. Most, because they are prevented from voting; others, because they choose not to. Almost inevitably, people on the city council will play to the people who vote, even though they may have sympathy for those who don't.

Let's look at one example. Rent control is overwhelmingly supported by Watsonville workers, who often pay more than half their checks for substandard, overcrowded, illegal housing. They have signed petitions in support of rent control by the thousands, and at a public hearing they turned out in hundreds to urge the new city council to control rents.

But when the issue came before the city council it was "sent to committee" where it was supposed to be silently buried. Not one member of the city council spoke for it. Off the record, the liberals explained that a rent control law would only lead to a recall election, where they would be thrown out and "all our recent gains" would be lost. Even Oscar Rios, proud defender of Latino Watsonville, said not a single word in defense of this measure which would almost immediately transfer money from mostly white landlords to mostly brown tenants.

LULAC's performance was even more discouraging. Right after the earthquake, in front of the old conservative city council, a LULAC representative spoke out strongly for rent control. But once the liberals took power and decided this issue was too hot to handle, LULAC, not wanting to do anything to embarrass their friends in office, let it drop.

During the Cinco de Mayo party I sat at the Watsonville Housing Action Committee's table with Francisco Juarez. I have known Francisco since 1977 when we cut cauliflower together at Valley Harvest (Valley Verga, we called it), and his story shows just how complicated these class questions can be. Francisco was born in Hundacareo, Michoacán, one of the small Mexican towns which regularly sends its men and women to work in the United States. He arrived in Watsonville in the early 1970s, along with his mother and father, worked in the fields from 1973-'84, and then in the local UFW office in those grim years from '84 to '89. While working during the day he attended night classes at Radcliff Adult School and Cabrillo College. He now works for the welfare department, daily delivering mostly bad news and diminished checks to impoverished Mexicans. His mother still works in the fields, and his father works in a nursery.

Francisco has a bright future. He is smart, handsome, thoroughly bilingual, and a hard worker. And yet he sits at the WHACO table, talking up the program that the Latino/Liberal alliance finds so inconvenient: rent control, an inclusionary ordinance which mandates low income housing, and airport conversion. Francisco, with one foot in professional life, but with the rest of his body and soul in the Mexican working class, knows that he makes no true advance separate from his own people.

He is not alone. The political direction of Watsonville's professional and semi-professional Latinos is not a settled matter. A rebuilt Mexican working class movement would attract many more people like Francisco to its side. And it is only such a movement — almost entirely lacking in contemporary Watsonville since the near death of the UFW and the decline of cannery worker strength — which would be capable of challenging the power of the real rulers of the city. That, in turn, would produce Latino politicians with the courage to take a firm stand for things like rent control. And then we would have true reason to celebrate.

(May, 1991)

125

(Daniel Stolpe woodcut)

18

Good Liberals and
Great Blue Herons

Every year I take a group of students from Radcliff Adult
School to Elkhorn Slough. This year I went twice, the
second time with another teacher, Sarah Ringler, and a group
of younger students, 15-18 year old high school and junior high
school dropouts, trying to make their way back into the school
system while maintaining some measure of self-respect.

They are fine, energetic kids. Many of them speak a
marvelous language, mixing Spanish and English in a rapid
fire delivery of jokes, lies, and insults, designed to emphasize
their internal cohesion and shield themselves from outsiders.
They face a grim future, with neither decent jobs nor housing.
But they are not without hope, and they seem determined to
have a good time — as much fun as they can despite their bleak
prospects.

Part of a four-car caravan, I drove a group of five young
women the six miles from downtown Watsón (as they call it)
over the Pajaro Bridge, out Salinas Road to Elkhorn Road and
the Elkhorn Slough visitors center. Like my own children, as
I chauffeur them around town, the students rattled on, oblivi-
ous to my presence.

"Oooooh, look at him, qué fine."

"He goes with Letty, la hermana de Enrique."

"Shit, I am better than her, que no?"

Matters of the heart are the constant theme. Life at school seems to be a tension between sexual energy and fear of being embarrassed in front of friends.

"Anybody been here before, heh?"

"In the fifth grade."

"What's it like, heh?"

"Fucking boring. No hay nada. Birds and water, birds and water."

Birds and water is what it was when Portola and his crew arrived in 1769. There was other wildlife too — wolves, elk, antelope, deer, rabbits, mountain lions, bobcats, grizzly bears, and coyotes — but what was most remarkable were the thousands and thousands of birds, in magnificent variety, drawn to the area by the extensive wetlands: a river that dominated the valley floor, many lakes, and a large system of sloughs that meandered from the foothills to the sea. These first European men to see Watsón were not unfamiliar with the pristine beauty of Native American California. Carefully, they named each place. What they saw here they called, *El Valle del Pájaro*, Bird Valley.

Despite more than 200 years of systematic draining, pumping, and filling of the wetlands, much of the water and many of the birds remain. And not just in the official sanctuaries like Elkhorn Slough. We still have five natural lakes, and an extensive system of sloughs — Hansen, Harkins, Gallighan, Struve, Watsonville — which, amazingly enough, sustain a fair amount of plant, animal, and bird life in our midst.

But not for long. Three major developments, currently marching towards city council approval, will effectively destroy the sloughs that remain within the city limits. The moving of the soil, the grading of the land, and the construction of houses and roads scheduled on the properties of Messrs. Jay Lohr, Mort Console, and Norman Schwartz, taken together, will do in the sloughs.

Some water will remain, just as it does behind Watsonville Square in Struve Slough on the east side of North Main, but water is only part of what makes up a slough, and the wildlife associated with it. The hilly grasslands that border the water are integral to the system that provides a home for rabbits, several varieties of mice, moles, voles, shrews, weasels, snakes, salamanders, and birds.

Building down to ten or twenty feet of the flood line may leave some water during the winter, but it does not protect a slough. If you want to see what will happen to the extensive wetlands on Watsonville's western border, take a look at the clogged bramble in Watsonville Slough behind Portola Heights, or glance, as you drive by on North Main, at the lone pair of egrets who sit behind Clothes Out, in what remains of the western edge of the eastern Struve Slough.

Many of the people who are making the decisions which are going to allow this to happen are reasonable liberals who pride themselves for their progressive attitudes and opinions. Why are they moving full speed ahead on these developments? They make one basic argument in their defense: we need to put low-income housing somewhere.

The argument stinks. The Jay Lohr "Villages" has plans for 136 low-income units, another 100 moderate-income houses if the new inclusionary ordinance is applied to the development, and some 900 expensive homes. Do the affordable units justify the project? Some progressives say "yes, a few units here, and a few units there, and it all adds up." Yeah, and a few acres of wetlands gone here, and a few gone there, and no more birds.

Moreover, there is no guarantee that the other two projects, Console and Schwartz, will provide any low-income housing at all. The new inclusionary ordinance, which supposedly would cover these projects, mandates only that the developers build 25 percent moderate income housing. We do need moderate income housing, but a little honesty please. In exchange for destruction of the in-city sloughs we get a large swath of expensive homes sold mostly to people from out of town, plus a good percentage of housing affordable to households making between 30,000 and 38,000 dollars a year, and a few low-income units.

Hard choices, you might say, but something has to give. We need low and moderate-income housing, and we need to preserve our agricultural land. Perhaps building to the edges of the sloughs is the least worst choice.

What makes this argument so infuriating is that not all the choices are being considered. What about the 290 acres at the airport? Closing the airport would allow us to build 1,500 units of moderate to low-income housing, a large public park, many mini-parks, and three schools, all the while protecting our agricultural lands and our wetlands. What would we have to give up? An airport that is primarily a recreational facility for the wealthy, and a handful of jobs directly tied to it.

If the city council is so committed to building moderate and low-income housing that they are willing to severely damage our wetlands, why aren't they willing to close the airport? Why are they going around town bad-mouthing airport conversion, while they supposedly wait for a report from the airport study commission? Could it be that the airport has a bunch of rich, powerful defenders, while the wetlands are protected by only a few environmentalists?

Mayor Todd McFarren and the liberal majority on the city council are in a bad fix. They have rejected as politically impossible a program that would have gone a long way to solving Watsonville's housing crisis: rent control, an inclusionary ordinance that mandates low income housing, and airport conversion. Proudly practicing the art of the possible, they are trying to build some low-income units without alienating the local real estate industry or scaring off the big developers.

But the "art of the possible" leads the liberals to a set of policies only slightly better than those of the reactionaries who used to control the city council. And it leaves the Watsonville housing crisis unchanged: thousands living in dangerously overcrowded conditions, most people paying way too much of their income for shelter, and developers continuing to use up what little land we have left as they build houses mainly for the rich.

The field trip went pretty much as expected. The students broke into small groups and continued their non-stop rapping as they trudged the three and a half miles of trail, with the visitors' center binoculars hanging unused around their necks. Now and then, something would catch the eyes of a few of them, and there would be an intense moment when they were distracted from their own lives. Those few moments were the point of the trip.

Rafael and Juan lagged behind with Sarah and me, actually using their binoculars and trying to identify the birds; we spent a nice little time together in a bird blind, trying to figure out whether we were watching a Curlew or Godwit. Meanwhile the others moved ahead.

Later we tried to catch up with them, as Sarah and I were embarrassed about how loud they were and over how far a distance we could hear them. As the four of us hurried along, a great blue heron glided into view, and for a few seconds all of us had him in our binoculars.

I do not have words to describe the sight. The large bird moved slowly, showing off his two-tone beauty: gray/white from his body out to the edge of his wings, trimmed neatly in cold blue. He swooped effortlessly across the water, his white and black head folded back against his shoulders, his long orange/yellow legs trailing behind. Choosing a spot, he slowed the ever so gentle movement of his enormous wings, extended his lovely long neck out from his body, and brought his legs forward with a majestic grace unknown to all but wild creatures. He came to a stop, making only the slightest ripple in the water. All in silence.

If development proceeds at its present pace, there will come a day in the lifetime of my students when people will not understand why this ever was called the Pajaro Valley. May it go in the public record that some of the damage was done when the good liberals, Todd, Oscar, Parr, and Lowell, held majority control of the city council.

(April, 1991)

.

Autobiographical Note

In the last 32 years, I have worked on eight "alternative" publications. The first was *The Wooden Shoe,* four pages of mimeographed polemics which Marvin Garson and I tried to sell for a nickle to Berkeley students in 1962. The title was an obscure bilingual joke: The word sabotage (we claimed) comes from the French word "*sabot,*" meaning shoe, and dates from the time when French workers protested the Industrial Revolution by taking off their wooden shoes and throwing them into the new machines that were ruining their lives. Of course nobody got the reference, and few were interested in our particular brand of political humor. *The Wooden Shoe* closed down after two issues.

Next came *Root and Branch,* also in the early '60s in Berkeley. Produced mostly by radical graduate students (led by Robert Scheer, Ruth Markovitz, and Maurice Zeitlin), this serious "little magazine" combined reworked graduate term papers with incomprehensible poetry and artsy photographs. The title came from the rhetorical wont of 17th-century English radicals who promised to make over society "root and branch," but I remember one perspective buyer who thought it was a gardening magazine. As the main editors had their eyes on bigger things than a little magazine (Scheer went on to *Ramparts, Playboy*, and the *Los Angeles Times*, while most of the others moved into academic careers), *Root and Branch* wilted and died after two issues.

Next was *STEPS*, its title even worse than the previous two. This was another little magazine, but now the year was 1967, and instead of being obscure freaks, we were in the center of a mass movement. *STEPS* was supposed to be that movement's "theoretical journal." But the typesetter was murdered in a bad drug deal, and we folded up shop after the obligatory two issues.

In the fall of 1968, Marvin Garson (of *Wooden Shoe* fame) started the *San Francisco Express Times,* a weekly tabloid that tried to build bridges between the political radicals of Berkeley and the cultural rebels of San Francisco. This was a successful publication (I wrote the sports column) with exactly the right feel for the express times we were living through, and it lasted a wonderful year and a half. But in the summer of 1969, after the batttle of People's Park, Marvin announced that the Revolution had been won, and now we merely faced the problems of post-revolutionary reconstruction, which didn't particularly interest him. So he changed the name of the paper to *Good Times,* and disappeared. The *Good Times* was bad news, and soon folded.

My journalistic endeavors resumed in 1972 in Salinas with *El Obrero.* No obscure titles now; we were straightforward proletarian revolutionaries. This monthly tabloid lasted two seasons until our five member collective split in three different directions, and I landed — feet down — in the friendly confines of Watsonville.

Next — it was now 1980 — José Lopez, Joe Fahey, and I started the *TDU Noticiero.* We used this regular sized newspaper and a series of leaflets to build the local chapter of

Teamsters for a Democratic Union. TDU did fairly well in Watsonville, and Joe is now president of Teamsters Local 912. But TDU as a local organization collapsed during the frozen food strike that it helped promote, and in Watsonville TDU came to be nothing more than three incomprehensible initials after Joe's name.

Then came *El Andar*, where most of the articles in this book were first published, and I had a good ride for about two years. *El Andar* began as a collaboration between students (mostly Mexican) from Cabrillo College and the University of California at Santa Cruz, and Watsonville radicals, both Mexican and Anglo. But when identity politics finally reached Watsonville in the early '90s, this joint effort was doomed. The Watsonville radicals were forced out/left the paper, one by one—I among them. Without a local connection, *El Andar* could not survive in Watsonville, and it moved to Santa Cruz, where it has been transformed into an almost exclusively Latino publication.

Currently, I am the joint editor — along with AV Coyle and Jane Crowley — of *Union Notes,* the newsletter of the Watsonville Adult Education Teachers' Union. No more mimeographs, we put it out on a computer and a copy machine. We have a circulation of 55, and we are damn good. Another mass movement surely lies ahead.

(October, 1993)